Still More

Secrets Of

SUCCESSFUL

Exhibiting

Strategies, Tips & Insights

To Make Your Exhibiting
Dollar Work Smarter & Harder

From

Some Of America's
Leading Professionals

Susan A. Friedmann • Dr. Robin F. Potter • Anne Barron
United Van Lines, Inc. • Robert L. Lapides • Don Woodard
Scott Tokar • Mark S. A. Smith • Hyla Lipson
Lorraine Denham & Brian Vanden Broucke
Lew Hoff • Timothy Polk

Secrets Of SUCCESSFUL Exhibiting

Compiled by

Susan A. Friedmann

Edited by: Timothy Polk, M.A., Santa Rosa, CA

Cover Design and Page Layout by: Ad Graphics, Tulsa, OK

Printed in the United States of America

Library of Congress Catalog Number 99-96520

ISBN 1-890427-06-3

Published by:

AVIVA
PUBLISHING

a subsidiary of Diadem Communications
P. O. Box 1850
Lake Placid, NY 12946-5850
(518) 523-1320

Additional copies of
Still More Secrets of Successful Exhibiting
can be obtained from any of the authors by calling
their individual number as listed with their chapter.

Quantity discounts are available.

CONTENTS

FOREWORD

This is the third edition of *Secrets of Successful Exhibiting*. While the first two editions have been very successful, this edition provides you an even greater level of industry perspective and in-depth knowledge. Collectively, these authors present you, the reader, with a shared perspective that would be difficult to find in most media; a perspective that will enlighten you in terms of exhibiting effectively.

By reading and understanding this book, you will be a better exhibitor. You'll gain insight into everything from shipping and logistics, to strategic planning and ROI, to successful promotion and staffing. You'll learn how to target your buying audience, track and manage leads for success. You'll understand how to use exhibits as a sales medium that generates bottom-line results. It's all here for the reading, in one easy-to-follow, efficiently edited publication.

Trade shows are big business. According to the Center for Exhibition Industry Research, there were 4,291 exhibitions in 1998, 110 million attendees, 1.4 million exhibiting companies, and 438 million square feet of exhibits. To be sure your company gets its slice of this pie, you owe it to yourself to be the best exhibit manager you can be. *STILL More Secrets of Successful Exhibiting* will help you accomplish this goal.

Michael J. Bandy
President, Trade Show Exhibitors Association

INTRODUCTION

Welcome to the third and newest installment in the *Secrets of Successful Exhibiting* series. Each of the twelve chapters inside have been written by an industry expert eager to share their knowledge, tips, and insights regarding the tradeshow industry. Each chapter focuses on a particular element of tradeshow exhibiting, including:

- Logistical pre-show planning for the tradeshow exhibit manager

- The "nuts and bolts" of exhibiting, including creating an effective booth, shipping, and lighting

- The "art" of exhibiting via pre-show and show marketing

- Utilizing the Web and other on-line opportunities to the fullest extent

- The effective use of hand-out materials, aisle-view presentations, and selling at the booth

- Post-show lead follow-up

Together this information comprises a virtual "beginning to end" handbook to help you stretch your exhibiting dollars, generate more leads and excitement at your booth, and—above all—turn your tradeshows into an effective vehicle to secure long-term repeat business from satisfied customers.

Good luck with your successful exhibiting!

Susan A. Friedmann
The Tradeshow Coach

SUCCESS

Secret #1

Empower Yourself Through Technology

by
Dr. Robin F. Potter

Empower Yourself Through Technology

Dr. Robin F. Potter

Technology and Trade Shows: An Oxymoron

The trade show industry has been arduously slow to embrace technology and move into the electronic age...despite the fact that today there are more than 1.5 million companies that exhibit their products or services at trade shows.

The Center for Exhibition Industry Research (CEIR) estimates that more than 350,000 companies exhibit an average of four times per year and that 98,000 companies exhibit at ten or more shows per year and spend more than $250,000. The trade show industry, in total, represents a $70 Billion a year industry. Additionally, trade shows captured nearly 17 percent of total spending on business-to-business marketing communications in 1997, up from only 10.7 percent two years earlier, according to the "Outfront Marketing II" study published Spring 1999 by Business Marketing magazine. Spending on trade shows ($12.6 billion) is quickly closing in on sales promotion ($13.6 billion) for the No. 2 spot in marketing budgets. Advertising ($17.7 billion) remains the top category.

What most people see at a trade show are the exhibit booths, the people representing the company, and the giveaways to attract potential clients to their exhibit booth. What is not seen is the tremendous amount of coordination and paperwork that is required by both the small and large exhibitors to enable them and their companies to have a successful exhibit at a trade show or event. Bare with me—the truth may hurt—but pre- and post-show paperwork and logistical planning is what the trade show manager *really* does. This is the reality of trade shows today.

The biggest culprit is paperwork. Paperwork is required to secure the space itself, as well as separate paperwork for obtaining electricity, carpeting, furniture, equipment, cleaning, catering, drayage, staffing, hotel, air transportation, rental cars, computer equipment, lead capture devices, floral, telephone (including Internet access) and many other services. Not only is this paperwork very specific, it usually is required for each item, staff member or tradeshow being planned. Furthermore, it is replicated for every exhibitor at the same tradeshow or event.

In addition to the paperwork required for attending the trade show or event, there is also the internal corporate paperwork required to coordinate the logistics of, among other elements:

- Staffing—who will be attending

- Transportation—getting people to and from the show

- Lodging—who will be staying where

- Shipping—products, the exhibit, promotional materials, etc.

- Budget—getting internal approval for employee and booth expenses

Had enough? The demands continue. Even more paperwork is required to: track shipping of trade show booth equipment, tracking of when deposits have to be made and when balances are due, scheduling the proper sequence of when artwork and signage should be finished, when to send out pre-mailers, when to contact outside vendors, speakers or VIP guests, etc. The amount of logistics and information required for a trade show can be overwhelming, and often results in increased costs due to late deposits, missed deadlines or inaccurate guarantees.

Although logistics and reports are demanding enough, there also is the time-consuming and logistical nightmare of submitting all the paperwork. Now most paperwork submission is done via Federal Express, Priority Mail, fax or snail mail; only a small percentage is submitted via the Internet.

"The details will kill you. It is the small things that can be forgotten or listed incorrectly that get you."
– Jennifer Williams, JCM Industries

Buried under an avalanche of logistics, trade show managers have made the best of a bad situation for a long time by using three-ring binders, file folders, sticky notes, and "homemade" Excel-type spreadsheets to track the hundreds of details involved in the exhibit management process. The cost-controlled, minute-by-minute, logistical orchestration of everything from people to presentations that nobody would even imagine are tracked. Then there are the pre- and post-show reports to be generated. Who should be where and when? How much did hotels cost? How do this year's expenditures compare with last year's? How are expenditures to date looking verses budget? What are the prepaids so far this year and next year?

The three-ring binder methods make it difficult to manage a single trade show, let alone several in a year. According to a May 1999 Tradeshow Week Poll, exhibits are an essential part of most companies marketing plans. However, logistics consume the largest portion of exhibit managers' time.

"83 percent of polled exhibitors said
they spend most to half of their time on
the logistics of their exhibit programs."
– May 1999 Tradeshow Week Poll.

Just think of the time and energy that is consumed on logistics verses implementation?

With the aforementioned paperwork and data management required of trade show exhibitors, producers (associations, show management companies and show producers), general service contractors, vendors and exhibit houses, it is obvious that there is a desperate need of solutions to decrease paperwork, save time and increase efficiency. The solutions so far have proven to be good paper organizers, but are not effective solutions with respect to the sophistication and amount of data required by the trade show industry. As well, the documentation and reports required by the managers, officers, accountants and staff within the company itself is growing. This often leads to extra cost, frustration, overwork, errors and an environment that is less than conducive to the task at hand. Trade show exhibit managers and producers are very vocal about wanting an electronic solution.

The Industry Wants and Demands a System That Will Accommodate Submission of Information Up To the Last Second, Not the Last Day or Minute.

What the trade show industry craves is very similar to what has occurred in the healthcare and banking industries. Figuratively and literally this means a system that will accommodate submission of information at the last second, not the last day or minute. Today on-line real time electronic submission of paperwork is the norm in healthcare and banking and soon will be in the trade show industry. Companies have invested heavily in technology and want their employees to utilize this technology to its maximum potential.

Why Have Electronic Solutions to the "Data-Management" Nightmare Been So Slow in Coming?

What have been the obstacles to electronic solutions to the present trade show "data-management" nightmare? Following the old adage, "If it ain't broke, don't fix it," the trade show industry has stuck to its old tried and true tools to make the best of the situation. Until recently there haven't been any great incentives to be more productive. However, as Wall Street has been buying up the trade show industry, productivity and Return On Investment (ROI) are now major incentives. The current system is old and slow and needs to be overhauled. As trade show industry executives watch Fortune 500 companies reap real productivity gains from the automation of mundane corporate transactions through software and Web-based applications this inertia will change. Steve Lohr, a business writer for *The New York Times*, in a May 1999 *Convene* article titled "Moving the Action From Desktop to Network" states:

> *"Meta Group, a technology research firm, studied many companies to see if they were getting a measurable payoff from their investment in Web-based systems. The answer was an unqualified "yes," with the estimated return on investment ranging from 20 percent to 800 percent!"*

Furthermore, until now there has been no software to act as the "footprint" or desktop solution to the exhibitor. Software for the desktop computer of the exhibitor that provides a location from which data may be sent or received. The trade show industry problem is similar to healthcare. Until the doctor had a practice management system in the office, literally on the desktop, there physically was no way to submit insurance forms electronically. The implementation of these systems enabled the Internet and electronic transfer of healthcare data.

Finally, confidentiality is a must. Trade show exhibitors, producers, vendors and exhibit houses want to be assured that their data is secure and remains confidential. Use of outside third parties will aid in providing the level of security and trust just as it exists in banking today.

What Software Is Currently Available?

Lead capture software, contact management software, meeting management software, and Internet based versions thereof have been available for some time. Recently, Internet enabled software for registration, housing, events and virtual trade shows have come to the market. However, all of these applications are partial solutions to a specific area of trade show exhibiting—none cover the logistical part of planning an event.

"None of the software out there specifically addressed the needs of the trade show exhibit manager."
– Alan Sherman, Schick Technologies

Specific resources for "partial solution" software are available via buyer's guides and web sites of industry associations and periodicals such as:

- American Society of Association Executives (ASAE)

- International Association of Exposition Managers (IAEM)

- Professional Convention Management Association (PCMA)

- Trade Show Exhibitors Association (TSEA)

- American Health Care Convention and Exhibitors Association (HCEA)

- Computer Event Marketing Association (CEMA)

Finally, Trade Show Management Software

Despite long-time obstacles to the development of trade show management software, the software is now available. In April of 1998 software was released that addresses the trade show management process and the multitude of details. With a sight to the future, a series of software products has been produced. The products include single user, network and exhibit house versions. The software effectively integrates many of the logistical areas required for exhibitors and exhibit houses. These include expenses, due dates, personnel information, housing, airfare, shipping, to do's and a comprehensive inventory, budgets and reports section. Graphics and Internet compatible versions are expected to be available late 1999.

"When I think back to life before TRAQ-IT, the first thing that comes to mind is that all of our trade show information seemed to be scattered everywhere...in binders, folders, spreadsheets, you name it. And even though we have our

own internally designed database of information at GTE for equipment, displays, available attendees and such it was never quite up to date with accurate information. I would spend a great deal of time trying to track down all the information that I needed to do my job and manage all of the multitude of details that are involved in planning a successful show."

– Jean Hale,
Communications Systems Division,
GTE Government Systems Corporation,
June/July 1999,
Tradeshow & Exhibitor Magazine.

Beyond remembering everything, the software has a comprehensive report generator. In an environment of downsizing, right sizing and pressure to produce more with less and have an improved Return on Investment (ROI) too, this software is a breakthrough in trade show management. This software is a terrific resource available to trade show managers and their companies to decrease paperwork, save time, increase efficiency and thus save money.

"Finally there is TRAQ-IT. It thinks like a trade show manager.

I have cut my preparation time for events by 85 percent. The savings in time have been incredible. It is so great to be able to enter information one time and then it is available as needed. Plus, I can keep a running tab on expenses which allows me to go to my superiors at a moments notice with accurate expense and budget information."

– Lisa Mills, Dymon, Inc.

The Future...Internet Enabled Trade Show Industry Clearinghouse

Electronic submission of the forms required for the trade show industry is very complex and integrated. The trade show exhibitor is not interested in submitting paperwork electronically for just a few of their shows, but is interested in submitting paperwork for **ALL** shows. The critical element for the electronic submission of forms for all trade shows is the implementation of a third-party trade show solution— an **Internet based solution** for the entire trade show industry.

TS One.com is an example that will soon come on-line. This Internet solution will allow the exhibitor to submit all their forms for all their shows. Using one Internet site, the information is forwarded on to the appropriate show manager or vendor (associations, show producers, show managers, official contractors, etc.). All of these transactions are done with total confidentiality and security. This Internet solution will become the "lifeline" of the trade show exhibitor allowing trade show managers to work from any location and at anytime with dedicated software and Internet connectivity.

To say the least, the exhibitor and the Internet solutions will become one. Once the trade show manager is using the desktop trade show management software and accessing the Internet in conjunction with all of their trade shows, they will become part of a true industry solution. An industry solution that is happening now!

What Does this Mean to You?

"Yes, Virginia, there is a Santa Claus!"

After years of waiting, thousands of miles of three-ring binders, and tons of file folders, sticky notes and home-grown spreadsheets (not to mention the frustration!), there is relief from the minutia. An electronic Internet-based solution to a very real data-management nightmare is emerging.... A solution that empowers the trade show manager to focus on strategy instead of details....

However, it is incumbent upon you, the exhibitor, manager or producer, to continually educate yourself as to what is available. Technology is moving at a geometric verses arithmetic rate. A year in technological and Internet terminology is two months chronologically. Move quickly to educate yourself technologically in order to become a consummate professional in your area of the trade show industry.

Take action! Don't let excuses or your travel schedule stop you. Get informed. Become involved with your professional organizations. Get your corporate executives involved in the movement. After all, the use of the available software and Internet enabled applications will only make you and your company more efficient, effective and guarantee a higher Return on Investment (ROI) ...all of which is "music" to most corporate executives ears.

Out of chaos comes change and opportunity. Empower yourself through technology.

Dr. Robin F. Potter

Dr. Robin F. Potter is a recognized visionary, futurist, authority and speaker in the area of electronic transactions and financial transactions, especially as they relate to healthcare, banking and tradeshows. Leaders in the healthcare, financial and business communities seek his financial and strategic advice. He has frequently been a quoted resource and speaker for numerous business journals and trade associations including *Investors Daily, Forbes, Wall Street Journal, Business Insurance, Exhibitor* and Trade Show Exhibitors Association.

Dr. Potter is best known for entrepreneurial healthcare, financial and software endeavors. He is the Founder of PulseCard, the first healthcare credit card in the United States. While Dr. Potter was President and CEO, PulseCard was named the fastest growing technology company in Kansas in 1995 and 1996 and was ranked #258 of the 500 on *Inc. Magazine's* list of fastest growing private companies. PulseCard's healthcare credit card was recently added to the credit card collection of the Smithsonian Institute in Washington, DC.

He also founded MSAver, the first Medical Savings Account (MSA) company using debit card technology restricted to healthcare. He was one of the leading proponents of MSA legislation that was adopted by Congress in 1996.

It was during this time that Dr. Potter saw the need in the trade show industry to have available a software program to automate the logistics of the exhibiting process. The experiences he gained from exhibiting at more than fifty (50) shows a year, in addition to input from numerous trade show mangers and producers, led him to build TRAQ-IT, a software company dedicated to the automation of all aspects of the trade show industry.

> *"The goal is to empower the trade show industry through technology."*
> – Dr. Robin F. Potter, President, TRAQ-IT

TRAQ-IT has received the coveted Buyers Choice Award at the 1998 Exhibitor Show and in 1999 was recommended by Inc. Technology Magazine as Best of Show Off the Shelf.

Dr. Potter also envisioned and designed an electronic, Internet-enabled solution for the trade show industry. In 1999 he founded **TS One.com**, the only trade show solution of its kind. The mission of **TS One.com** is to provide integrated Internet solutions to the trade show industry, while at the same time becoming the recognized market leader and solution provider to the trade show industry.

He was recently appointed to the Joint Internet Task Force of IAEM and TSEA to "advance the use of the Internet in the events industry."

For more information contact:

TRAQ-IT
...Tradeshow Software Solutions

P.O. Box 12221
Overland Park, KS 66282-2221
Phone: (913) 498-1221
FAX: (913) 345-2466
www.traqit.com
www.TS ONE.com

If you are the person who coordinates your company's trade show efforts, click over to www.traqit.com. This Website for trade show software introduces you to a tool for planning, managing and overseeing the hundreds of details and minutia of tradeshow management.

"TRAQ-IT helps me manage all of the steps, tasks and details that are involved in exhibiting at trade shows. It's like having an assistant that just works and works and never takes time off!"
**– Jean Hale,
Communications Systems Division,
GTE Government Systems Corporation**

SUCCESS

Secret #2

Integrated Marketing Rules!

by

Lorraine Denham and Brian Vanden Broucke

Integrated Marketing Rules!

Lorraine Denham and Brian Vanden Broucke

In rock 'n roll, Elvis rules. In the space program, John Glenn rules. In coffee, Starbucks rules. In science, Einstein rules. In computers, Microsoft rules. In casual attire, The Gap rules. In films, Spielberg rules. In fashion, the little black dress rules. We could go on and on. In any industry, any field, any entity there is usually one defacto standard by which all others are measured. You may not agree with our choices, but in their fields they stand out as excellent and exceptional.

In trade show exhibiting, Integrated Marketing Rules! Integrated Marketing is the defacto standard, the supreme status quo, the Elvis of exhibiting! Because IM works better than anything else in marketing at trade shows. Period. End of discussion. But the start of a new game plan.

"Integrated Marketing" has become a buzz phrase in the trade show industry for some time, yet very few truly understand it; and even fewer execute Integrated Marketing programs successfully. Nonetheless, the benefits of Integrated Marketing have been shown time and time again to breed winners where others have failed.

Benefits

Integrated Marketing's consistency increases learning. Today, your customer is virtually overloaded with information. According to research, *the Sunday edition of the New York Times contains more information than the average 18th century person was exposed to in their entire lifetime.*[1] We are besieged by thousands of mes-

---

[1] Data Smog-Surviving the Information Glut; Daniel Schenk

sages on a daily basis while sadly catering to a society with an MTV attention span. We now talk in "sound bytes." Frankly, we just can't take it all in anymore.

- **Integrated Marketing projects stability and builds mindshare.**
  A company that has built strong market awareness through successful branding has already gone through the experience of defining themselves (and spent a pretty penny to do it.) It never ceases to amaze us why major firms abandon all that equity and effort when it comes to trade show marketing to start buying into gimmicks and goodies.

- **Integrated Marketing saves time & money.**
  As a disciple of Integrated Marketing, you become a champion for your company by intelligently leveraging internal resources. These resources in most cases are already pre-approved and easy to expand creatively and thematically. Also, with the size of marketing departments being what they are, and deadlines getting tighter and tighter you don't have the time, energy or resources to re-invent the wheel for every show (nor should you want to.)

- **Integrated Marketing makes connections that build business.**
  It just makes sense—from building stronger brand awareness to increasing message retention to amortizing investments—your customer will take notice. But how do you get from here to there?

To begin with, Integrated Marketing at trade shows is more than just putting out more of what you have done before. You need to extend your core values. The ultimate goal is to penetrate deeper into the brain of your customer, moving them from conscious thought to sub-conscious thought (where they know who you are without really thinking about it.)

Avis Rules!

Avis is demonstrating how Integrated Marketing Rules with their new ad campaign. Dozens of years ago, when they were behind Hertz as the number one rental car company, they repositioned perceptions by using the powerful and successful theme "We Try Harder."

With their growth, they could easily have done what other companies have done and change their positioning out of their own internal boredom or belief they had to "update." Avis however just "extended" their message with "Technology doesn't try harder, people do. We Try Harder For You."

The five "rules" that make integrated marketing **rule**:

1. Know your **A**udience.
2. Focus your **M**essage.
3. Be Specific with **O**bjectives.
4. Extend Marketing **R**esources.
5. Create an **E**xperience.

Rule #1: Know your Audience.

There is something very basic that all exhibitors have in common with their trade show audiences—we are all human beings! How convenient. We're appealing to creatures that are essentially just like us regardless of them being engineers, doctors, architects or undertakers. Companies don't sell products and services, people do.

We buy because we have needs. But more importantly, we buy because we have wants. I need a car—I want a BMW. And all things being equal, we will buy from people we like versus people we don't.

Nowhere else does the power of people more deeply influence a sale than at the trade show, where your Integrated Marketing message continues seamlessly from the ad, to the brochure and web-site to a full-living, breathing and sensing environment. Trade shows are a unique three-dimensional marketing venue which attendees can experience and enjoy while building a strong interpersonal bond with you.

Everything you do to market on the show floor should be aimed at fulfilling these innate customer wants. Something we learned a long time ago—clever doesn't sell. Every time you come up with a bright idea, no matter how dandy it may seem at the time, ask yourself if your audience will care. If the answer is "probably not," it's back to the drawing board.

Rule #2: Focus your Message.

The message is King and we are all slaves to it. It's easy to get caught up in the excitement, pizzazz and variety of modern communication toys, but you need to remind yourself what you trying to say. Once that is done, the fun can begin! Of course, a simple look at a company's annual report will net all kinds of poetic missions and messages. But let's dig deeper.

Human beings retain only 50% of what they hear and 90% of that is forgotten in one minute or less — so you must keep it simple. Begin with one over-arching message. That one message becomes your rallying cry or theme. It provides the creative glue; the consistency that holds your project together from beginning to end. Collateral, promotions, signage, presentation content—everything emanates from this place. The more organic the message (one that is in keeping with your core values and/or what differentiates you from your competition) the better.

Under that main message, you may have one to three sub-messages. But that's it! The late James Fixx said: "The less information the mind receives the more it wants to participate." And participation (interactivity) with your audience is key.

Finally, people only remember things that are meaningful to them. Product Managers may demand a gargantuan sign to reside over their widget extolling its many illustrious features. Simplify this eye pollution at all costs. Fight, fight, fight to minimize copy in your booth!

In summary, to win the battle for message mindshare at trade shows, forget about communicating how your products work, and tell them how it's going to work for them. Define your differentiators that save them time, earn them more money, make their lives easier, create a sense of security or take away the pain—that's really all that matters.

Rule #3: Be Specific with Objectives.

It's amazing how many projects are started without a clear set of objectives. There are really only four things you can accomplish by exhibiting at a trade show:

Build Image
Drive Leads
Gather Market Research
Educate People

Be sure to prioritize those objectives numerically. Have everyone on your team participate and gather a consensus. You've got to know what you want to get out of your project before you can begin to measure success. It's analogous to getting into a cab and saying to the driver "don't take me to Omaha." The response of course would be..."well, where the heck do you want to go?"

Be as specific with objectives as you possibly can. For example:

Leads. #1 Goal. We want 1500 leads. Of that, we want 20% to be qualified. We know the leads are qualified if...(Set parameters.)

Image. #2 Goal. We want everyone visiting our exhibit to know we are a player and why. (Set parameters: smartest, biggest, most sophisticated, best value, etc.)

Market Research. #3 Goal. We need real-time customer data to understand...(Set guidelines.)

Education. #4 Goal. We want our attendees to realize our depth of product/service benefits. They are ...(define)

Now, when it comes to measuring results, you now have a benchmark that can be evaluated and corroborated.

Rule #4: Extend Marketing Resources.

Integrated Marketing means leveraging promotional equity you already possess in-house and combining it with fresh marketing material. That doesn't mean just re-using what was left of last year's giveaways. It means creatively re-purposing anything and everything that is in-line with your current message—white papers, videos, commercials, ads, etc. Naturally, fresh marketing involves creating new and exciting ways of saying the same thing. However, major corporations routinely devalue a company's corporate identity with marketing programs that are based upon "creative for creative's sake" or gimmicks rooted in pop culture. The art of Integrated Marketing is re-inventing excitement without re-inventing the wheel.

Very often too, the timeline to produce trade show marketing is drastically compressed. What one used to be asked to do in six months now is expected in 6 weeks or even 6 days! We scramble for new this and new that—ideas, images, etc. without taking the time to brainstorm more "holistic" concepts. The result is a hodge-podge of impressions. Remember, if your prospect cannot instantly identify who you are and what it is you do, integrating your marketing will be a moot point.

Rule #5: Create an Experience.

This is probably the most essential integrated essential of all. There is nothing more powerful than creating an experience with your marketing program. There is no question how valuable presentations, promotions, multimedia and the like can be in garnering results—but one cannot expect them to work magic alone.

Integrated Marketing is the inventive and creative combination of communication tools to create a powerful, significant experience that your audience will be impacted by and remember. This starts with a dynamic idea that brings your message to life, and stimulates your audience's senses. They become surrounded by your message and can feel the spirit and essence of your company. The value is that you have reached them deeper and they grow more involved and committed to your cause.

And it all starts with a great idea that brings your message to life!

As an exercise in doing that, during brainstorming work with your team and vendors, make sure your provide everyone with lots of paper and have a write board, or large pad of paper for all to see. Start by asking everyone to create one paragraph about your company in a general, overall way. Whatever comes to mind immediately is usually best. When everyone is done, go through the results and assimilate the best into a group paragraph. Make sure this one paragraph is visible for all to see on a write board. (This one paragraph should not be far from your branding, or mission statement.)

ONE PARAGRAPH:

"We are a stable, leading edge technology company that delivers more than promises. We work in cooperation with our industry partners and work collaboratively with our customers in a full-service support structure. We have a vision for the future with a firm commitment to quality research, product design and continual excellence. No other company can compete with our depth of products, or our approach to providing products that benefit our customers."

When everyone is happy with that, ask the participants to distill that one paragraph down to one sentence. We know this is tough, but this is how you find the energy in your company.

ONE SENTENCE:

"We are a stable, customer-focused company that works collaboratively to deliver products with excellence, and supports with a full-service approach."

From that one sentence, pick out one action verb to provide energy. (This exercise can be repeated and may go in an entirely different direction.) Put that one action verb in the center of a large piece of paper. This will become your mind map to new ideas.

ONE ACTION VERB:

"Collaborate"

WORD ASSOCIATIONS:

From that one verb, find other synonyms that express the same action...

"Collaborate. Work Together. Join Forces. Concur. Cooperate. Combine."

WHAT PEOPLE DO THESE THINGS?

Then on another level of the mind map, list the people who do these things...

"Musicians, Synchronized Swimming, Chorus's (vocalists), Construction Workers, Office Staff"

WHAT PLACES ARE THESE THINGS DONE?

List the places these things are done...

"Offices, Train Stations, Music Halls, Sports Arena, Schools"

WHAT DO YOU EXPERIENCE WITH THESE THINGS?

And the things you might experience when the action verb is activated.

"Excitement, Fun, Toe Tapping, Hand Clapping, Heart Thumping, Awe, Joy"

SENSE ASSOCIATIONS:

After that, make "sense associations" of how you could smell, see, hear, and even taste these actions. What you'll eventually have is a non-linear road map that should stimulate creativity and bring your message to life in more exciting ways at a trade show.

Make some choices now and begin to pull different ideas from the mind map and put them together. You'll be amazed at the variety of directions your creative concept can go while remaining true to your core values. The beauty is they all came from your message, so they'll be ideas that are organic and easy to implement. And they'll work!

Bringing sensations to your message is how you bridge humanness to a cold corporate mission, and thus begin to create a total experience that involves your audience. In the process of building your ideas from improvisation to detailing to execution; you are capturing their senses; stimulating their thinking and reinforcing messaging they already know. Your marketing programs will also be more powerful because they will be experiential, human and integrated.

A commitment to the rules of Integrated Marketing means that your company will rule with results like never before. Your trade show program will rule with smart, powerful ideas coming to life in your exhibit. And you will rule. You will become the standard bearer, the trend setter, and the keeper of the flame. Everyone wins when Integrated Marketing Rules!

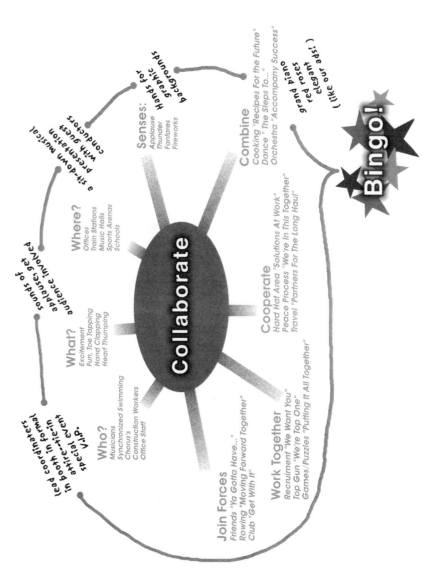

In brainstorming a corporate concept, lay out all ideas on a write board starting with your One Action Verb as the center. Draw all ideas around it ala a "mind map." As you can see in this illustration, the word "collaborate" leads to a great theme—Accompany Success; and a complete trade show concept.

Lorraine Denham and Brian Vanden Broucke

Lorraine Denham and **Brian Vanden Broucke** are the Co-Founders of Unipro Marketing Services, a national company that pioneered Integrated Marketing in 1992. Since that time, they have produced hundreds of marketing programs for small start up's to the Fortune 1000. Their work has won many awards, most recently a Sizzle Award for Best Integrated Program in 1998. Other clients include: IBM, Xerox, Unisys, Hewlett-Packard, Lucent and Federal Express to name a few.

Starting Unipro allowed Brian and Lorraine to develop a close-knit business family that would share their vision of resourceful preparation, unlimited invention, and demanding standards of excellence. Together, the people of Unipro built a company culture based on their shared values of Integrity, Honesty, Courage, Respect and Creativity. Brian feels, *"the process is as important as the final product. And we are all committed to quality, responsibility and a 100 percent success rate."*

Brian and Lorraine are dedicated to their industry and are involved in many associations to provide education and validation for trade show professionals. Their company was a key player in starting a Bay Area chapter of TSEA, and Lorraine is the Communications Coordinator for the Windy City Chapter of TSEA. Lorraine believes, *"being an integral part of building a trade show community is very important to us at Unipro. We are in a people-oriented business; and by strengthening connections we all learn, grow and benefit."*

In addition to overseeing their busy production schedule, Brian and Lorraine are both popular and dynamic speakers. They are proud of their six year relationship with The Exhibitor Show, speaking on a range of topics, including Integrated Marketing. They have also authored literally dozens of articles that spread the gospel that "Integrated Marketing Rules."

Lorraine lives in a historically preserved area of her home town Chicago in a lovingly renovated Victorian home. Her personal passions are her friendships, her art collection, and her nine year old son, Elliott.

Brian lives in a small, yet tasteful crater on the moon where the air is unpolluted and Cable TV is not available.

For more information go online to:
www.unipromkt.com

Or call us at 1-800-Y-Unipro

SUCCESS

Secret

#3

Internet Strategies for Better Exhibiting

or

*How the Web Can Dissolve Space and Time,
Save You Money, and Make Your Exhibit
a Rousing Success*

by

Robert L. Lapides

Internet Strategies for Better Exhibiting

or How the Web Can Dissolve Space and Time, Save You Money, and Make Your Exhibit a Rousing Success

Robert L. Lapides

A recent CEIR report indicated that making contact with a prospect in the field costs $997, but only $550 at an event. By using the Internet strategically, you can get that cost-per-contact down even lower. The Internet can help you make better planning decisions, build a better booth, promote your presence, and extend that presence well beyond the show floor. Here are just a few of the ways that exhibitors have been using the Internet to make the most of their trade show investment.

Selecting the right event

Staging a successful exhibit at a major trade show is a complex process that involves lots of time, planning, and money. You want to do it right, but within budget. The first step is to find those events where your products will be seen, heard, touched, tasted, smelled and, hopefully, purchased by the most promising prospects. Rather than passively sifting through piles of incoming mail and trade magazines, you can actively search the Web for the types of events most likely to bring out the buyers.

That five-pound directory of trade shows is probably out of date by the time it's published. Internet sites, by contrast, can be updated whenever information changes, several times a day if necessary, so you are more likely to find up-to-date event listings on the Web.

Surely, the popular general search engines and directories—such as AltaVista, Yahoo!, or Excite—can get you started. Sooner or later, one of these search engines will point you to a dedicated online event directory. These sites maintain comprehensive, up-to-date directories of trade shows and other events and some allow you to search by event name, topic, industry, and date, as well as location. With these dedicated search engines you can narrow your search quite effectively and finish with a sense that you have surveyed the major shows for your industry.

As you search, you are likely to uncover information about current and past exhibitors at each show so you can keep on eye on your competition and be sure that you are showing up in all the right places. More and more trade shows have their own Web sites, which you can also browse for more detailed information.

Build a better booth and they will come

Your booth is a symbol of your entire company packed in a 10 ft. x 10 ft. or even 40 ft. x 40 ft. space. So, you'll want to devote some creative energy to your booth space. And since booth costs typically consume approximately one quarter of your event expenditures, you'll want to spend wisely here.

As in real estate, the first three components of your booth are location, location, and location. If you wind up in a shadowy corner of the floor, or if you are situated next to a more well-heeled competitor whose booth dwarfs yours, you have a problem. Professionals recommend walking the floor of the building where you plan to exhibit, but this is seldom practical. Here again, you can turn to the Internet for help.

An increasing number of shows let you view an electronic blueprint of the trade show floor, with booth locations and exhibitor names clearly visible. With a few mouse clicks, you can zoom out for a bird's eye view of the show floor to get a general idea of where competitors, entrances, exits, and amenities are situated.

These online floorplans can also offer you an opportunity to promote your show presence. Many organizers are creating full online events and online event directories to complement their physical shows and exhibitor guides. Be sure to look for opportunities the organizer offers to highlight your company in the "virtual show." Maybe you can include a hyperlink to your company's Web page and a logo instead of just your name and booth number.

Find suppliers online

Once you secure your booth space, the arduous task of outfitting your exhibit begins. Typically, this means plowing through the Yellow Pages and last year's files to locate exhibit designers, promotional item suppliers, consultants, contractors, shippers, and so on. Before you're done, you'll be awash in a sea of yellow stickies.

Now you can use the Web to streamline that process considerably. Many online event directories also let you search through lists of suppliers dedicated to making your trade show a success. A few clicks will yield a long list of suppliers for each item you need. In many cases, you can even order what you need right on line.

By now, you should be familiar with an emerging theme: the Internet oils the wheels of commerce, making transactions and communications smoother and often faster. By venturing on line to contact suppliers, you can do more comparison shopping more quickly, send RFPs easily, and bring home the best deal in the least time.

So why is communication via the Internet better than a phone call? It isn't always, but telephone conversations require both parties to be connected at the same time. Sure, you can play telephone tag, but that's primarily an exercise in frustration. You can send an e-mail to a supplier, or place an order online outside of regular business hours and they will have all the information in writing, and you will have a "paper" trail in case anything goes wrong.

To repeat the mantra: Being able to make inquiries and place orders online saves you time and money.

Book flights, hotels, and cars online

So far, you've used the Internet to find best events, checked out the competition and your booth space, and communicated with suppliers to order what you need.

Now you have to get you, your equipment, and your staff to the big event.

Where else to turn but the Internet? Travel Web sites offer numerous conveniences and savings to the business traveler. Without leaving your computer, you can locate the most economical and convenient flights, choose your seat, book your tickets, and even rent cars at your destination point. Some of the online event directory Web sites also enable you to book your travels directly from their site. Similar online purchasing options are available for car rentals and hotel rooms.

Promote your presence online

After you've arranged for your booth and have your travel plans in place, you are ready for another absolutely necessary step. You need to promote your exhibit, and then promote it again.

You can advertise in the traditional print media, such as trade magazines and show guides geared to your audience. But it will also pay to advertise in the electronic, Net-based media. After all, chances are good that your prospects are spending more time on line these days and less time flipping those glossy and expensive trade magazine pages. Of course, many trade magazines now also boast a dynamic online presence.

Bring them home with banner ads

By placing a banner ad on a targeted Web site, you can reach your prospects quite effectively. Banner ads offer tremendous benefits. They are relatively inexpensive, for starters. What's more, you can track exactly how many people see them and how many times users click on them.

On Web sites with search engines, banner ads can be triggered by the keyword that a user enters on a search form. Suppose a prospect searches a general Internet directory site like Yahoo! for information on "antiques." If you were an exhibitor specializing in antique watches, your banner ad could be displayed when this keyword was entered, and you would be billed accordingly.

By placing your banner to pop-up when key words are entered in an *event-related* directory site, you qualify your prospects even more directly. If you are exhibiting at the annual MSSYI (Most Significant Show for Your Industry), you might buy a banner promoting your presence every time someone searches for information about the MSSYI show or keywords related to that show. Chances are good you will be reaching someone who is planning to attend MSSYI, or at least a very viable target for your branding messages.

The Net is all about links to people, places, and sites. It's all about streamlining communications and eliminating the middleman. By setting up hyperlinks on any Web site where your prospects are likely to gather, you can get qualified leads to come to you directly.

Even better, consider that leads that reach you through hyperlinks are pre-qualified. These prospects actively sought out your site. With a little interactive querying, you can qualify your prospects even more precisely and then direct them to the offerings on your site that they will be most interested in. As you learn more about a prospect's preferences, you can direct him or her to just the information they need. Note that you are moving to a form of one-on-one communication that the Internet enables so economically.

The Internet is a marketer's paradise that bestows a level of precise feedback that advertisers until recently could only dream of. It is a relatively easy matter to record precisely how many people visited your site, at what time, and from what link. Moreover, setting up hyperlinks is a remarkably economical way to get prospects to come to you. Compared to the hefty printing and postage costs associated with traditional information packets, it's an amazing bargain.

Beyond the show floor

One downside of events is that after the huge investment of time and money poured into planning, outfitting your booth, training floor personnel, promoting your presence, and purchasing travel and hotel rooms, the actual event is over in just a few days.

After the teardown, you are left with sore feet, stacks of business cards, and crates ready to be shipped home. Once again, the Internet can help by extending the reach of your event in space and time. Both before and after the show, webcasting—broadcasting streaming video and audio over the Internet—can enhance your physical show presence.

Before the show, a video or audio webcast on your Web site can pique attendees' interest. You could audio webcast a personal invitation to your booth from a company executive, or webcast your latest product video with a special voiceover inviting prospects to stop by your booth to see the new developments.

At the show, a webcast from your booth might be used to demonstrate your products, unveil an important technological development, or report news of a strategic alliance. With a webcast on your Web site, you can reach those prospects that were unable to come to your booth and give anyone with an Internet connection the chance to see the great things you did at the show.

Webcasting from the show floor can also help you justify your show budget, as it gives others in your company, who typically don't attend your trade shows, the chance to see the huge crowds you attracted with that great new booth, the dynamic presenter you contracted, and the lavish product unveiling you organized.

Virtual booths

For years, technological prophets have espoused the notion of "virtual reality," a kind of simulated world that lets people experience various actions, such as flying a plane, without incurring the cost, danger, or expense of the actual event. Well, virtual reality is an actual reality on the Internet today.

Today, you can set up a "virtual booth" that allows prospects to tour your booth from the Web, learn about and interact with your products, read testimonials, or enter a contest.

There are many companies that can help you produce these "virtual booth tours." From their computers, prospects could examine your booth with a click of the mouse. You can offer prospective customers a 360-degree tour of your entire exhibit space including interactive portions they can click on, such as webcasts, surveys, and even product demonstrations. Click on the photo of a computer screen and an interactive demo is launched, click on the photo of the plasma screen and your corporate video plays, click on the link that says "product brochure" and your brochure is e-mailed to them automatically. The possibilities are *virtually* limitless!

Get started today

Of course, webcasting, virtual tours, and other Internet developments will never replace the flesh-and-blood reality of an actual trade show. Nothing can match the chemistry and energy of face-to-face meetings with your prospects. But the Internet can be a cost-saver and efficiency tool for planning, promoting, and extending your show presence. The Internet, which oils the wheels of commerce, simplifies business processes, and dissolves space and time, can make the process of exhibiting much easier for you:

- As we've seen, you can start using the Internet to search for events and check out the competition.

- You can surf the Net to find the best suppliers to outfit you with an attention-grabbing booth.

- Without leaving your keyboard, you can search for the cheapest airfare or car rentals and the most suitable accommodations.

- You can use tools unique to the Web, such as banner ads, to advertise and promote your event.

- You can extend the reach of your show in space and time by producing webcasts of your products or a key speech by your company's president.

Internet technology is here now and it can enhance your planning, promotional efforts, and execution at every stage of the game. But it's up to you to put it to use. Just reach for your mouse, hop online, and you're on your way!

Robert L. Lapides

Robert L. Lapides is founder and CEO of TSCentral, Inc., the leading provider of online information, products, and services for the trade event industry. Before founding TSCentral in 1995, Mr. Lapides founded and served as Managing Director of World Access Corporation (WAC), based in Wellesley, Mass. For more than 10 years, World Access was a leading organization in the field of international trade event representation, promotion, and management. The firm represented over 300 events covering more than 40 major markets and more than 70 industries annually. Among its many achievements, the firm was recognized by the U.S. Secretary of Commerce as the leading firm assisting U.S. companies in participating in overseas trade events via the Department's Trade Fair Certification Program.

Prior to WAC, Mr. Lapides was Assistant Managing Director of OmniHolding A.G., in Zurich, Switzerland, where he was responsible for a portfolio of business enterprises owned by OmniHolding, primarily in the international trading services industries. He went on to become Executive Vice President and Treasurer for OmniSwiss Properties Ltd. in New York, NY. There, he was responsible for all financial negotiations and performance of a portfolio of real estate development projects valued at over one billion dollars.

Mr. Lapides sits on the boards of directors of several international companies and institutions and is a frequent speaker on subjects related to e-business, the trade events industry, entrepreneurship, and international business development.

TSCentral Q&A

Who is TSCentral?

TSCentral is the leading Internet-based provider of information, products, and services for the trade events industry.

Event organizers, exhibitors, industry service providers, and attendees rely on TSCentral to help them plan and participate in events efficiently, and generate new business.

What does TSCentral offer?

- www.tscentral.com—The best Web site for finding trade shows, seminars/conferences, venues, industry suppliers, and event webcasts
- Professional webcasting services
- Online events and virtual booths
- Internet marketing opportunities
- Floorplan management tools

What can I find on TSCentral.com?

The most extensive international listings of:

- Trade shows
- Seminars and conferences (including online registration!)
- Suppliers to the events industry
- Venues and Facilities
- Convention and Visitor's Bureaus
- Webcasts from all the industry events

And more!

What's webcasting and how is it used?

Webcasting is broadcasting video or audio over the Internet. It's a great way to leverage your company's investment in trade shows and tie your trade show programs in with the rest of your marketing programs.

Imagine filming your product demos or new product unveilings then broadcasting them live over the Web to reach a worldwide audience. You could also distribute them to your sales force on CD, or send them out to prospects through direct mail.

What does the TSCentral web page look like and how do I find it?

Designed to be easy to use, the TSCentral Web site can be found at <u>www.tscentral.com</u>. You can search for events, venues, and suppliers right off the home page or browse by industry to find news and events directly related to your market.

How can I contact TSCentral to get more information?

TSCentral
110 Cedar Street
Wellesley, MA 02481 USA
Phone: 781-235-8095 Fax: 781-416-4500
E-mail: info@tscentral.com
Visit us on line at: www.tscentral.com

SUCCESS

Secret

#4

Handouts and Giveaways that Get You Business

by

Mark S. A. Smith

Handouts and Giveaways that Get You Business

Mark S. A. Smith

A key element to exhibiting sales success is your literature strategy: how you use brochures, fliers, and sales collateral at your show. What is it that you hand to show visitors? How do you make it effective? How do you make sure that you're not wasting your money?

At most shows, you see two different literature strategy camps—the "load'um up" people, and the "give'um nothing" people.

Literature Can Kill Sales

If you sell a complex product, just handing out literature can hinder the purchasing process. If a prospect reviews the literature and doesn't find what they're looking for, they may think that you don't offer what they want, and then you're disqualified. In this case, it's more important to have a product expert talk to your prospect and find out their needs on the spot than have them misinterpret your literature later.

Take No Literature

Those with experience use literature sparingly. They feel that if an attendee is burdened with literature, it doesn't get home. It will end up in the trash at the show or in their hotel room. Ask yourself, what good does their huge shopping bag of literature do for you?

You may choose to not take literature to trade shows. If you have limited funds and staff, you may prefer to have the literature-only collectors keep walking. Having no literature keeps your exhibit clean and professional looking. You eliminate the literature clutter typical in most exhibits.

If you offer a 250-page hard-bound, 4-color catalog, don't pass it out at the show, ship it to them after the show is over. And you can use it as an offer on the show floor.

You may ask visitors to order the literature that they want. Promise to fulfill the request quickly, and keep your promise. Arrange to fill their request by the time they return from the show, or at least within three or four days after the show. You now have an excuse to talk with them after the show. "Did you get what you expected? What did you like best about it? How can I help?"

Bring Some Literature

If your product is easy to understand, bring the best and most appropriate literature for the show, and display sample copies. Train your sales people to review the details of your products from the literature, and use the customer's interest in your literature to secure leads you can close.

This works best when your literature is a brief overview of your product, when it's a reference and a reminder. You can increase the success of this strategy if you ask the visitor to hand it off to the person responsible for making a buying commitment.

You may wish to store your literature where people can't get to it. If a visitor asks you for a brochure, you can reply with, "We have lots of brochures. I want to make sure that I give you the right material so you can decide to buy from me. What do you need to feel confident to make a decision?" Their reply will tell you how serious they are about buying and tell you what you need to give them to make them say yes to you.

Create a Show-Specific Brochure

Given the cost of attending most shows, you may find that creating a targeted promotional piece for that particular audience is a good investment. You can create a piece that's concise and targeted to the buying criteria of that group. If the visitor needs your more-detailed literature, you can give them a copy on the spot or send them what they need after the show closes.

Developing Literature that Works

When you develop keep the decision maker in mind. What are they searching for? What do they need to know that they're making the best decision? How will they decide? Is the decision made by a team, or an individual? What are the criterion being considered? What will you use the literature for?

Unfortunately, many companies still write their sales literature in a customer-less vacuum, with no input from the sales force or from buyers. Savvy companies take a more aggressive approach. They use testimonials from customers. They ask, "Why did you buy from me?" That becomes the basis for their sales pieces.

If you have multiple markets, create a tailored brochure for each market. Use examples, case studies, and photographs that you buyer will instantly relate to.

Because you user's decision criterion varies, you need different approaches for each market. For some buyers, the decision focus is low-cost. So write a brochure with the focus on cost benefit. It may be that those who purchase your product consult others before making a decision. In that case, your literature supports the team approach. For some buyers, the critical question is, "Does it work? Does it produce the desired effect. Is it easy to use?" If that's the case, you have to meet and demonstrate that you can.

Giveaways That Work

Premiums and incentives have been a part of the trade-show business since the very beginning. Visitors' offices are littered with pens, coffee mugs, note pads, and other trash and trinkets they collected at trade shows.

You've been to shows, swiped goodies from the candy jars, collected your bag of trash and treasures, and then taken them home either to throw them away or give them to the kids. You may have noticed that the number of freebies given away at trade shows is way down. Here's why: what impact did these give-aways have on your buying decision? Right! Most exhibitors have learned that freebies to the masses don't deliver increased sales.

Some professional-association shows prohibit certain giveaway items like food, candy, newspapers, posters, T-shirts, bags, and novelties. Ask show management what you're permitted to do before ordering 10,000 imprinted Frisbees®.

Why Giveaways Turn Visitors into Thieves

Freebies can deter sales. When you set up a candy bowl or offer other free-for-all giveaways, you actually turn your visitors into thieves. You've seen them: they sneak up, snitch a piece of candy, and slink away, avoiding eye contact. If you do make eye contact, they say "hi-how-are-you" and move away at full speed.

A candy bowl really doesn't bring buyers into your exhibit, and it takes up valuable exhibit space. An exception, of course, is if you *sell* candy and you're giving away samples.

When you're offering cool gifts, how many times have you been asked, "Can I have another for my kids?" You have to say yes or you look like a jerk. Then the person asks you what you do, and you end up doing your pitch to someone who is really only interested in your freebie.

You visitor takes from you something more valuable than your "gift." Your exhibit is costing you thousands of dollars. When someone takes five minutes to ask you about what you sell so that they feel better about taking your giveaway, they've taken far more than the cost of the gift, they've taken away irreplaceable time that you could have spent with real buyers.

Giveaways That Don't Get Business

If your giveaway doesn't bring you customers, don't use it. If you choose to use a giveaway, make sure that you're trading the prize for your visitor's name, address, phone number, and buying criteria. Get the information your sales staff needs to close the sale.

Select items that reflect the quality of your company. You don't want your logo on a cheap pen that doesn't write. One of the dumbest giveaways is bottles of water. It doesn't even leave the show floor and the trashcans are littered with the sponsoring company's logo. There is a subconscious discounting of who you are when a prospect throws away something you've given them.

Giveaways That Get Business

The giveaway should be something genuinely useful, and it should be kept in a place where the prospect will refer to it when the need for your product arises. A good example is the Domino's Pizza refrigerator magnet. You come home, find nothing in the fridge, and call Domino's delivery. If you can't position your giveaway effectively, don't use it.

The best premiums are those that help your visitors get their jobs done faster or better. They are things that visitors wouldn't necessarily buy for themselves, but would make their life better. They have a high perceived value and cost you very little to reproduce.

Information has the highest perceived value and the lowest relative reproduction cost. For example, reprints of articles, special reports, audio and videotapes, computer software, and books related to your field. These premiums *self-select* your prime prospects, because they are of little use to people who can't buy from you.

An effective premium is a laminated card that slips into a wallet, covered with valuable reference information that your customers use regularly. For example, a Century 21 office in Denver gives out a three-fold city street guide that doubles as a business card. A welding-equipment distributor gives out wallet cards with recommended amperage settings for welding a variety of alloys.

One of the most effective promotions we've ever used is a laminated wallet card that includes the *Trade Show Success Checklist.*[1] It includes valuable information that any trade-show exhibitor will need, it's a reminder of what we do, and the contact information is discretely included, so that clients can easily contact us with their questions. (You can also listen to the audio program, 7 Steps to Trade Show Success at http://www.guerrillagroup.com.)

Tools make excellent giveaways. For example, hand out a dive table card for scuba enthusiasts, or a plastic slide rule for landscapers who need to calculate application rates for fertilizer. Another example is a wine

---

[1] Call 800-247-9145 for your free copy.

selection book for a meeting planner, or a keyboard-mounted calculator for a computer programmer.

Some organizations only use incentives if they have a new product release or a new application, and then it's closely tied to the product.

Hide Your Goodies

Insist on making your giveaway work hard to get you sales. If you decide to use premiums, keep them hidden, and use it as a parting gift. Say, "Thank you for stopping by. Here's something for you to take with you as a thank you for your time. We'll talk after the show." They'll take your follow-up call.

Make Visitors Earn It

Qualify visitors with a controlled giveaway. People will stand in line for T-shirts, hats, and sunglasses. Ask the visitor to complete a survey or a questionnaire, or have the visitor listen to a presentation to qualify for the prize.

No Bag Wars

Don't get caught in the Bag Wars, where others give away better-quality bags than you do. So you move up to more expensive bags, and they counter with even more expensive bags, and then, what's the point? Bags seem attractive for two reasons: everybody wants one, and they become walking billboards. The problem is that they fail the duel criteria for *self-selection* and *utility* after the show.

Why not avoid bags and containers altogether! The only really effective bag promotion we've ever seen was when United Parcel Service distributed specially designed bags, offering to ship them back to the visitor's office at the end of the show—for a fee!

Promotions that Waste Your Money

Avoid gimmicky promotions like pop the balloon or miniature golf because they waste time and money with people who will never do business with you. What's the relationship between a visitor's desire to ply mini golf and buy from you? Unless you sell golf equipment, it's the wrong choice.

Perhaps you've seen these acrylic grab-the-bucks boxes with cash blowing around inside. This type of promotion will attract everyone. That may be appropriate for your business, but more likely, you're just blowing your cash.

How to Collect Buyers

If collecting names for your mailing list is one of your marketing goals, hold a drawing to give something away. Consider giving away smaller prizes more often throughout the day versus a bigger, single prize at the end of the show. More visitors will drop their name and address in your fishbowl when they think there is a reasonable chance to win a prize.

If your show goal is to collect the names of all the visitors, consider not going at all and instead, buy the registration list. If it's an association show, either rent the membership list, or get it when you join. You may be even better off skipping the registration list and buying a good, proven mailing list to your target customers.

Unqualified giveaways mean you collect unqualified leads your sales force won't follow up. Unqualified leads come from giveaway items that attract every visitor, whether they can buy from you or not.

Draw for something that is only interesting to visitors with whom you can do business. Never give away things that are of general interest, like stereo equipment, travel, cameras, or TVs. Here's a test: if your sales people would like to take the prize home, it's a prize that won't necessarily attract buyers.

Contests that Select Buyers

Contests should *self-select* for qualified prospects. At a consumer electronics show, two competitors were both selling refurbished toner cartridges. The first vendor put out a fishbowl with a sign, *Drop your business card to win a* COLOR TV! The competitor put out a fishbowl with a sign, *Drop your business card to win a* FREE TONER CARTRIDGE! If you were selling toner cartridges, which stack of leads would *you* rather take home?

As a professional, lawyer, physician, accountant, consultant, or trainer, you could give away an hour of your services. Yes, you'll get some unqualified leads, but the number will be much lower than if you were giving away a Hawaiian vacation.

As a sporting equipment company, give away nine holes of golf with your owner or president.

If you're in the automotive industry, give away something that has to be installed by you, so the winner has to come to your shop, or your dealer's shop, to get it. Then you have a chance to sell them more.

At smaller, specialty conferences, you may want to consider having a drawing for various levels of prizes, including airfare, room and board, and registration fee for the next conference. That way the incentive brings the winner back to next year's show.

Pick Your Winners

Since this is *your* contest, *you* get to make the rules, and while a fishbowl may imply that the drawing is random, reserve the right to strategically *choose* the winners to help achieve their marketing goals. You might choose to have your top ten customers win, or your top 50 prospects. To be perfectly ethical, you may even choose to have *everyone* win. Use the winning notification as an opportunity to contact a buyer.

This chapter was adapted from *Guerrilla Trade Show Selling*, by Jay Conrad Levinson, Mark S. A. Smith, and Orvel Ray Wilson, published by John Wiley & Sons, New York, published 1997.

Mark S. A. Smith

Mark delivers innovative, unconventional strategies for entrepreneurial thinkers, marketing managers, and sales professionals to rope in the customers that looked all but impossible! Mark co-authored *Guerrilla Trade Show Selling*, *Guerrilla TeleSelling*, and *Guerrilla Negotiating* with Orvel Ray Wilson and Jay Conrad Levinson. He has written more than 300 articles on sales and marketing topics. He's an electrical engineer, computer programmer, hardware salesman, and software marketer who now coaches others how to get more business by being more than "just another salesperson." Mark believes that your sales performance can be every bit as reliable as the performance of your company's products. And after hearing him, his audiences agree.

His excellence recognized by his peers, Smith is past-president of the Colorado Speakers Association. He is a partner of The Guerrilla Group, Inc., conducting The Guerrilla Selling Seminar® for audiences nationwide.

Mark conducts workshops, delivers powerful keynote sessions, and creates custom information products for discerning clients, worldwide.

If you want to find out about other books and products to help you maximize your trade show success, go to http://www.guerrillagroup.com. There you'll discover articles, listen to audio programs, and find many resources that will be valuable for you.

Get your free Guerrilla Selling Tip of the Week. Sign up at: http://www.guerrillagroup.com/formst.htm

E-mail: mark@guerrillagroup.com. Mobile phone: 800-789-0150. The Guerrilla Group Inc. Office: 800-247-9145

"Why Should I Hire a Guerrilla to Train My People?"

Our clients tell us that they hire us again and again because our programs are...

Completely Customized to Fit Your Business

"It was obvious that you really did your homework. You understand our company, our competition, and our unique challenges. Half a dozen people asked me how long you have been one of our vice presidents."

Entertaining and Engaging

"Wow! Hysterical delivery with tons of content. I haven't laughed that hard at a comedy club."

Loaded with Secret, Unconventional Ideas

"Even our jaded, heard-it-all-before veterans are excited about using your out-of-the-box ideas."

Practical Weapons and Tactics that Work Magic

"This was no airy-fairy theory session. You delivered practical ideas we could use immediately."

Veteran Professionals are Easy to Work With

"I loved how you helped us with the technical aspects of our event. Because you do this a hundred times a year, your attention to detail saved the day."

Inclusive Fee Means No Surprises

"We loved knowing exactly what the program would cost. And I only had to write one check!"

New Audio-Video Technology Captivates Your Audience

"Your animated graphics, sound effects, and music added a real showbiz dimension to the training. It would have cost us more than $1,000.00 for us just to rent the equipment that you brought with you."

Motivates Your People to Act

"You turned our sales team into a formidable, fast-moving strike force. We closed 43% more business in the last 30 days."

What's it Going to Cost?

"We have measured the return on investment of our sales meeting at 2,000 percent. Even Internet stocks don't deliver that kind of return."

Most requested topics: Guerrilla Trade Show Selling. Guerrilla Selling: New Unconventional Weapons and Tactics for Increasing Your Sales. Guerrilla Teleselling: New Unconventional Weapons and Tactics to Close Sales When You Can't Be There in Person. Guerrilla Negotiation: New Unconventional Weapons and Tactics to Get What You Want. Customers Come to You: Unconventional Marketing that Works. The 5 Steps that Make Your Trade Shows Pay Off. Connecting With Your Customers: How to Do Business When You Only Have a Minute. Presentations They'll Remember Long After You're Gone. And many other marketing, sales, and customer service topics.

SUCCESS

Secret #5

Design Is Not Decoration

by
Don Woodard

Design Is Not Decoration

Don Woodard

A successful drama director once made the comment, "You never build the set, then create a play to compliment it." This statement is quiet relative to the exhibit industry.

For an exhibit designer to properly serve your organization, that person must understand what they are attempting to accomplish *before* they begin. Prior to creating your successful exhibit design, the designer will need to understand your company's exhibit marketing goals and objectives.

Years ago, I created a definition of a trade show exhibit that I would like to share now:

> *Trade show exhibit: An environment in which to make people aware of your products and services, and to educate and influence them in a positive manner to accept your offering at some point in time.*

I refer to this definition often not only prior to creating a design, but after I believe the solution has been discovered. If indeed the solution does meet the objectives—establishes an identity or presents the organization and its products and services in the appropriate light—then I will proceed with that creative thought. Remember, design is not decoration, it is a process to create a desired response.

To help clarify the strategic message you want the exhibit design to present, I encourage you to perform a simple exercise. Draw a line down the middle of a sheet of paper. On the left side write as many adjectives as you can to describe your company. On the right side, write all the adjectives you can to describe how you wish others would perceive your organization. This is a simple way for you to see the difference between "what is" and "what you want to be."

An exhibit designer is someone who can represent your adjectives and ideas through three-dimensional structures, textures, colors, and other visual and auditory means. Only space, budget, and time constraints limit the designer.

When creating a new exhibit or refurbishing an existing one, the designer must consider two creative dynamics:

What does the exhibit need to say?

How does the exhibit need to function?

What the exhibit needs to say is primarily an image or identity statement. Form, texture, color, etc., are among the many important elements to be considered. How the exhibit is going to function focuses more on logistical considerations, such as traffic flow, ease of set-up and dismantling, shipping, storage areas, and of course proper display of products.

Both creative dynamics need to be designed in relation to your specific sales and marketing goals and objectives. To maximize success, the trade show program should simply be an extension of your marketing plan.

There are three basic categories of information that your company can present at a trade show. They are:

- Company Identification
- Company Position
- Product Position

Company Identification is a method to explain or identify to show attendees what your company can do for them. Often this method is used to distinguish different product areas or services. This is a good approach for new companies that have not yet established a company image.

Company Position emphasizes an image or identity that your company wishes to portray. This approach is often used to position a company in its marketplace. Currently, many companies use this approach to position themselves as global players or as an industry leader.

Product Position is a method used to showcase the company's offerings. Company name becomes secondary. This method is a good way to present the benefits of using your products or services. (Always remember that people buy benefits, not products!)

After you have selected the desired "category of information," ideas on how to establish and present your strategic message will begin to emerge. As an exhibit designer, I feel that "how the exhibit needs to function" must be addressed before creating "the image" that the company wishes others to perceive.

Logistical considerations are numerous, including:

- What is the life expectancy of the exhibit? How many shows and in how many different configurations will the exhibit need to serve?

- What is going to be displayed? Are actual products going to be displayed, and if so, what physical dimensions do these have (height, weight, size, etc.)?

- Are there going to be working models or product presentations? Are workstations required? If so, how many?

- How many people will each product presentation address? Will they be one-on-one or group presentations? How much space do you wish to dedicate per presentation area?

- Is the exhibit going to be primarily graphics?

- Is storage within the exhibit a concern? If so, what will be stored and how much space will be needed? Does the booth staff need to have quick access to the storage areas?

- How is traffic going to flow? How are the show attendees going to move through the exhibit to maximize their learning experience and time? Do you want visitors to be guided through the exhibit, or can they be allowed to linger or browse on their own?

- Are you attempting to make your exhibit inviting for all show attendees, or do you prefer to be more selective in attracting pre-qualified visitors?

- What light requirements are needed? Do you wish to utilize lighting as an attraction element, or simply use lighting to highlight your booth and graphics?

- How does your company view installation and dismantling of the exhibit? Do you prefer to have company employees do this, or hire outside help? How much of a budget do you have allocated for labor (if any) per show?

- Have you considered the costs incurred with shipping, drayage, and storage? (These costs are often not considered in the early stages of exhibit design.)

After the designer has answered most, if not all, of the logistical questions, then the focus should be shifted to, "What does the exhibit need to say?"

Presenting an image or identity can be a bit trickier than offering solutions to logistical concerns. First, review your company's collateral materials. Do they represent your company as it wishes to be seen? Either good or bad, collateral materials may be of value to your exhibit designer—as long as you identify in advance which you like and those that you do not. Also, providing photos of previous exhibits, advertisements, and other company marketing materials will assist your designer.

Color selection is an important element when enhancing or creating an image. Should you use your corporate colors in your exhibit? It's often done, although many times it is more appropriately used as a highlight color. Red, for example, is an emotional color; too much of it can turn people away. Blue is a calming color. Nearly ninety percent of the Fortune 500 companies have blue in their logo. Males respond well to blue. If your buying audience will be predominately male, blue would be a good color to use.

Other color tips include:

- Yellow is the best attention-getting color.

- Green represents positive feelings and is also a calming color. Mixed with brass, dark green is an indicator of quality.

- Teal and purple are current "in" colors. However, be careful because eventually these colors will be considered "out," dating the exhibit.

- Black represents power. It is an excellent background to highlight colorful graphics.

- Gold, silver, and platinum symbolize quality. If your products are top of the line, these colors will enhance their value.

- White represents honest and purity. An all-white exhibit is a definite attention-getter because it is so unusual. White, however, is difficult to keep clean and generally requires a great deal of maintenance.

- Pastel colors offer a welcoming affect. Many companies switch from harsh, bold colors to pastels when doing an image makeover.

When selecting your exhibit colors, be aware of where you plan to exhibit. For international shows, confirm that your selections will not be offensive colors to other countries.

Texture is another prime image element. Should you use smooth or textured surfaces to represent your company? It will depend on what image you are trying to convey. Does your marketing plan utilize a theme? If so, textured surfaces are excellent ways to depict themes.

Many laminates offer marble, granite, and other rock-type finishes. These textures convey images of stability and permanency.

Brass, gold, silver, copper, etc. are very good accents. They say "quality and expensive." Do not use these if you are selling a low-priced product, as it will send the wrong message.

Fabric finishes are the most common exhibit textures. Fabrics that offer Velcro compatibility present many advantages for applying graphics and many colors are readily available.

Exhibit form is another important element when influencing your qualified prospects and customers. Sharp, ninety-degree corners present a much different look and feel than a ninety-degree radius curve; curves are friendlier than sharp corners.

Unusual shapes always draw attention because they are unexpected. It is the natural curiosity of humans to look at something that is unusual.

Many exhibits today including hanging fabrics. Often these materials are hung from metal truss systems, which present an interesting architectural element. Soft, flowing fabric mixed with hard, bold, metallic structures present an interesting contrast.

It is critical to have several key people within the organization review the design to confirm that the visual image is making the correct statement. Color, texture, and form all need to be working together to make your company's strategic message successful. Allow your exhibit designer to make recommendations, but be certain that your company's key personnel agree. (Or, at the least, that no one is offended with the design concept.)

An exhibit structure can make a bold statement about your company. It can represent aggressiveness, boldness, cutting edge, high-tech, and so forth, or it can say conservative, low-key, risk-free, etc. The uniqueness of a trade show exhibit is that it is your environment: you can represent your company in whichever way you desire.

Another major influence in the design of your exhibit should be who are your customers and prospects. To maximize your success, you should present your company to address the needs, wants, and desires of those who will buy from you.

Understanding who your buyers are will greatly enhance the success of your exhibit. For instance, what is the primary concern of upper management in almost every company? The bottom line or net profits!

So if your buyers are upper management personnel, your exhibit design and graphics have to address how your offering will effect your buyers' net profits. If your customers are sales management personnel, you will need to address how using your products or services can help increase sales.

Production managers are most interested in how your offering will increase their productivity or increase efficiency. Administrative personnel are generally looking for ways to reduce costs and save money. Distributors, on the other hand, are usually most interested in net profits.

Your exhibit signs and graphics need to be designed to address the needs of your customers. In addition, what and how your booth staff say should reinforce this concept to maximize results.

Always remember this: you should be building an "information source" for your customers and prospects, not a monument to your company. After all, what other venue do you have where your customers and prospects will spend their time and money to come see you?

Don Woodard

Don Woodard has been providing unique exhibit and sign solutions to customers for more than twenty-five years. His creative style has worked for both large and small companies. He is the president of Laarhoven Design/ Colorado, an affiliate company of Laarhoven Design, based in Atlanta, Georgia.

Laarhoven Design offers a full range of portable and modular exhibit systems to fulfill your exhibit needs. From basic table top displays to complete custom designed in-line and island exhibits.

Laarhoven Design has distributors and showrooms throughout the United States and Europe to provide you with a full-service exhibit network. From design to construction, set up and dismantle, storage and rental, Laarhoven will provide you with successful exhibiting solutions.

It was the concern for his customers' success that drove Don to initiate an educational trade show seminar more than nine years ago. This well recognized program has become a monthly habit for many exhibit managers, marketing and sales personnel, and a growing number of Colorado companies.

The value received from the trade show seminar programs has led to many speaking engagements, as well as authorship of numerous articles in various trade publications.

In addition, Don's unusual career path—from professional race car driver to sign painter to exhibit designer and builder—has provided him with an entertaining yet informative and motivational keynote program titled, "How to Successfully Build Your Business by Discovering the Secrets of the Hawaiian San Pit."

For additional information on educational trade show seminars or a keynote presentation to your group or organization, contact Don at 800-574-7318 or ldcdon@aol.com.

Laarhoven Design
7100 N. Broadway, Bldg. 5-H
Denver, CO 80221
www.laarhovendesign.com

SUCCESS

Secret

#6

Taking the Mystery Out of Fiber Optics Used for Graphics and Signs

by

Hyla Lipson

Taking the Mystery Out of Fiber Optics Used for Graphics and Signs

Hyla Lipson

In today's MTV-world, there is a new emphasis on the visual in general and lighting in particular. Fiber optics is a key way for an organization to make its booth not only more attractive, but also stand out from others.

WHAT IT IS

When we first began working with fiber optics in 1984, little was known about its use for anything, let alone something visual. Even after explaining its structure, folks seemed mystified. But fiber optics is actually quite a simple concept. The angle at which light bends when it passes through an object is called its refractive index. A plastic fiber optic strand is made up of two separate materials: the core and the cladding. The core has a higher refractive index (or angle at which light bends) than the cladding. This creates a barrier for the light, and it must bounce along the length of the fiber until it reaches an opening in the cladding. Plastic fiber is referred to as PMMA or polymethlmethacrylcate.

There are three major forms of fiber optics in the marketplace today. The first is end-lit fiber. This means light enters one end of the fiber (the input end) and travels the length of that fiber until it reaches the part that is viewed (the output end). This form of fiber is also called "point to point" since graphics are created using a series of dots. The second form of fiber optics is called edge-lit or linear fiber. The cladding in this fiber has been degraded, allowing light to leak all along its length. The effect is a glowing strand much like neon. And, finally, there are fiber pegs. These are pegs that are dyed different colors and backlit with fluorescent lighting.

Lighting a fiber optic strand means putting a bulb of some sort (typically a halogen lamp) at the input end. By introducing a color wheel in between the bulb and the fiber, one can change the color of light passing through the fiber. As the wheel moves past many fibers, consecutive action occurs or what we call implied motion. Changing colors in a directional fashion over various graphics causes the animation created with color wheels. Fiber elements *can* be turned on and off—either by turning the bulbs on and off or by placing black on the color wheel.

Fibers can be obtained in various diameters. The sizes are generally referred to by stating their diameter as a fraction of an inch, such as *.020" diameter*. The most popular sizes range between .010" diameter (very hair fine fiber) to .120" diameter fiber (very thick rigid fiber). There are other large core diameter fibers, although these are generally used for lighting and will not be discussed in this chapter.

The size of the fiber used for a display depends on many variables such as viewing distance, indoor or outdoor applications, detail, and budget. Fiber pricing increases geometrically from one size to another. Thus, a sign using 1000 .030" diameter fibers (.030" diameter is the most widely used and cost effective size) would cost about $875. The same sign with .060" diameter fiber would cost about $1,475. A reputable fiber optic fabricator can determine what is the best fiber to use in displays.

The lamps used to light fiber optic graphics are varied. As we stated earlier, halogen is the most common. A 50-watt halogen lamp is a perfect choice. Its color temperature provides a very white light that transmits through colored ink or gels to provide excellent matches for almost any pantone shade. The average life of a 50-watt halogen lamp has been increased to around 5000 hours. This means having to change lamps only once every 6 months or so if the sign is left on 24 hours a day. The lamps are 12 volt and require very little electricity so they are extremely cost effective to use. Most small signs require only 1 amp of electricity. Larger signs—say, a fiber optic wall containing up to 10 individual illuminators—will still only require 10 amps to power.

Another element of a fiber optic illuminator includes a synchronous motor and a transformer, which converts line current (120V or 240V electricity) to the 12 volts required by most of the components.

The color wheel is probably the most creative portion of the display. Custom handmade wheels utilize theatrical gels for the color. These are now made from polyester so they will not fade or deteriorate over time. Silk-screened wheels are made using special UV retardant inks and last years and years. The color wheels themselves are made of acrylic or polycarbonate.

We have now described the fiber optics themselves and the illuminators. The rest of the story depends on the application and the graphics. We now know that the input end of the fiber is considered the end connected to the illuminator. The output end is the visible part of the display. The output end is placed into a substrate of some kind. This is done by drilling holes in materials such as plastic or wood. Fiber strands are inserted into the holes and then glued in place. The loose end (the end that will become the input end) is then bundled so the light will pass over the fibers in a directional fashion creating the correct sequencing of a display. Since fiber occupies space and illuminators are set up to handle a certain number of fiber strands, sometimes more complicated displays require more illuminators. These may have to be synchronized. These can also be made to interact via buttons or laser discs or other form of "triggering" devices. Sound can be added and a multimedia event can be created. The sky is the limit! What you can dream can be rendered using fiber optics.

FIBER OPTICS FOR EXHIBITING

You have chosen the tradeshow(s) for the exhibit. You have carefully chosen the booth location for high visibility. You have purchased or fabricated the best possible booth the budget will allow. Now, is there a certainty that show attendees find the booth and, even more important, remember the company the booth represents?

It has been proven that lit and moving displays command more attention than non-lit, non-moving displays. A fiber optic sign, by its very nature, will afford the powerful combination of a name in lights that can change colors giving the illusion of implied motion.

Further, because of a phenomenon called "retina retention," a fiber optic sign is brighter from a distance. It is meant to be seen across the room. Retina retention is a process your eyes and brain go through in an attempt to connect the dots—the actual fiber points making up the name or logo.

This is similar to resolution in printing or photography and the gathering of pixels. This factor also helps "tone down" the visual as an attendee approaches your booth: the sign that was screaming to be noticed from across the room is now a rather quiet presence. It will not detract from your staff or materials to be viewed.

Test retina retention for yourself:

- *Hold the end of a pen between your thumb and index finger.*

- *Move your thumb and index finger back and forth, making the pen move quickly up and down.*

You will see an echo of form creating a fan shape where the pen has been. This is your eyes and brain at work trying to make sense in a chaotic world.

A few do's and don'ts when using a fiber optic sign for a tradeshow header:

- Do make the graphic large enough to be seen from a distance.

- Never turn the name of the company off. Change its color or animate the logo icon, but don't risk someone walking by at the very moment the name is off—even for a brief moment.

- Do enhance the logo and name with vinyl or other printed graphics if there is a concern about "off-axis" viewing.

- Don't think that fiber optics is synonymous with *glitzy*. Very sedate corporate logos and names can be created without appearing as if they belong in a casino.

- Do be creative and blend fiber optics with other forms of traditional signs. Cutouts, metal lettering, vinyl, laminates—all are possible and add to the final design quality of a display.

A note about viewing angles of fiber optics:

When fiber optics first were used as a form of sign, people complained about the "viewing angle." A fiber optic emits a cone of light that allows viewing for about 60 - 120 degrees total, which means that if a person is directly to the side of a fiber optic sign, the person will not clearly see what it says. (That's also true of most signs.)

There are things that can slightly increase this angle, but it is the feeling of most fiber optic companies that signs are meant to be seen in a fairly direct manner. Placement of the signs then becomes more important.

Photographics Used in Fiber-Optic Displays

In order to put fiber optics into a duratrans or C-print, a rigid surface must be provided. There are two options available for this process.

In the case of a duratrans which will be backlit AND enhanced with fiber optics:

The duratrans is mounted BEHIND a piece of acrylic or Plexiglas. The thickness is dictated by the overall size of the image. That puts the acrylic on the front surface, and the display can then be worked with and easily cleaned without harming the duratrans.

The mounting process, called dry mounting, must "marry" the duratrans to the acrylic. A clear adhesive is applied to the face of the duratrans, the duratrans is placed behind the acrylic, and both elements are put into a press, which tightly seals the two together.

Usually it is a good idea to bake the acrylic or Plexiglas prior to mounting to avoid "outgassing," which causes bubbles to form between the plastic and the duratrans.

The duratrans is dry-mounted on TOP of the acrylic. Then a matte protective coating is also dry-mounted on TOP of the duratrans. This is more complicated, requiring three pieces of material instead of the two in the other method; however, this is sometimes more desirable since it eliminates the glare from shiny plex.

In the case of a C-Print or photo mural which will NOT be backlit, but which WILL be enhanced with fiber optics:

(Note: The mounting process is similar to that with a duratrans.)

A C-print may be mounted behind plex; however, this will not create a totally opaque image. Some light from the fiber optic illuminator will reflect. Instead, mount the C-print on top of masonite or Sintra. Then mount a matte protective coating on the C-print to prevent soil or damage to the print. This is definitely the preferred method of mounting since it creates a totally opaque surface.

A few notes about what happens next:

It is usually desirable to receive a mounted image from the client or exhibit house. This allows total control over the image itself. Once the fiber optic company receives the image, the fiber optic graphics are developed.

The display is treated just like any other: holes are drilled, fibers are inserted, and finally all of the fibers are glued to the substrate or faceplate. Usually the entire back is "floated" with epoxy creating an even overall layer.

A note about Duraflex material:

Duraflex is a very flexible, durable photo-image material. It can be backlit or lit with ambient light so it can act as either a duratrans type or a C-print type image.

A note about sources of images:

There are a number of Stock Photo sources available. The price of the image is based on the use of that image. For tradeshow purposes, you will be asked how many shows will utilize the image. This is an incredibly rich source of ideas and graphics.

Interpretive Displays

Interpretive displays tell someone something. In the tradeshow environment, these types of displays can be the difference between someone just visiting your booth or someone really "getting" the point. It is a way of demonstrating a complex or critical idea easily with the use of movement and color.

There are many examples of this type of display:

- **Purina**—graphically described the manufacturing process of dog food in a tradeshow display.

- **Royce Corporation**—displayed the process of solid waste management in a professional tradeshow venue.

- **Peregrine Foundation**—illustrated the migratory paths of five species of predator birds at their interpretive center in Idaho.

- **Delphi**—lit various elements of an automobile's electrical system during an auto show in Europe.

- **American Bible Society**—showed the spread of Christianity in the world since the beginning of time for their home office in New York City.

- **FAA**—defined the many logistic systems at the Mike Monroney Visitors' Center in Oklahoma City.

Each display must be accurate, concise, and interesting. The use of fiber optics is a key factor in providing this interest; and because an event is created in the mind of a viewer, memory retention of the display is enhanced.

Maps used as interpretive displays:

Maps seem to be ever popular and for good reason: They can demonstrate communication, a national or worldwide presence, site locations, channels of distribution, districts of operation, and so on. There are almost limitless choices as to how to provide the original map, including:

- C-print or Duratrans enhanced with fiber optics

- "Plain" face with no graphics—everything is done in fiber optics

- Airbrushed graphics enhanced with fiber optics

- Vinyl graphics enhanced with fiber optics

- Metal or other material shapes enhanced with fiber optics

Factors contributing to the choice include budget, size, complexity, and time frame. Before a fiber optic map can be quoted, all of these factors must be considered and then the nature of the project is revealed and discussed:

- Should there be linking lines in one direction from point-to-point?

- Should each line be a different color?

- Are there multidirectional communications that must be demonstrated?

- Is this to be interactive or will it cycle on its own?

- Are there to be future changes?

The actual locations on a map should be provided full size to a fiber optic company. A client knows best where everything is. Another person's guess might not be as accurate. Fiber optics are not really a changeable medium. Adding or subtracting locations can be difficult and expensive. It is best to plan ahead and create the most accurate display possible in the original manufacturing process.

Multiple Image Displays

Used to display a graphic and a logo

This is an interesting way to superimpose a logo and a name. Many companies have used this technique when their name changes or when they merge with another company. First, one logo appears, then another. And, to make the displays last longer, they can be set up to eventually shut down the old logo so only the new logo appears.

Used as a "magical" element

This includes the surprise factor! One image is on, then it disappears and an entirely new image appears. Since fiber points, which are not lit, do not show up, especially with the use of fancy laminate faces or the addition of smoky plex over a face with lots of fiber, what isn't on is totally hidden. Magic!

Various means of cycling the images

- One image can appear from left to right. The next image can also appear from left to right and seem to "sweep" away the original image.

- One image can remain on for a set amount of time. Then by turning off that bulb and turning on another bulb, the next image can "snap" on.

These two types of cycles can be mixed and matched for additional special effects. The variations are mind boggling!

There seems to be a special language connected with fiber optic signs and displays!

Single Line Letters—A single row of fiber dots creating the curves or lines of each letter; a good choice for very small words or large amounts of text.

Outline and Infill—A letter outlined with fiber optic points with the space in the center of the letters either a random pattern or a regular matrix pattern of infill. Best used with larger letters as small letters will cause the word to blur and make legibility difficult.

Directional Color Flow—The manner in which a word will change colors. Common terms are "top-down," "left to right," "bottom-up," and so forth.

Magic Dust or Random Color Flow—A few fibers in each letter light in a new color, then a few more and a few more, until the entire letter or word is revealed in the new color. This is a magical form of changing colors or having an element "evolve."

Don't Leave That Display in a Crate

After the show or in between shows, display a fiber optic sign in your corporate headquarters. Everyone will enjoy seeing what is the latest and most interesting form of signage today in the marketplace. You'll be amazed at how much attention a fiber optic sign will really bring.

Summary

This was a brief overview of some of the ways to use fiber optics in exhibits. There are many other "enlightening possibilities," and we hope you will explore them all!

Hyla Lipson

Hyla Lipson is the founder and owner (with her partner John Jones) of Fiberoptic Lighting, Inc. Hyla began her fiber optic career in 1984. Since that time, the process of using fiber optics for visual displays has developed into a viable alternative for signs and graphics.

Choosing a fiber optic company to fabricate a project for any use is difficult because there are few standards to follow and everyone claims to have the BEST system.

The advice Hyla would give is this:

- Find a company that is at least 10 years old.

- Be certain the illuminators are UL, CSA, and/or EU listed.

- Ask for references of clients who have had similar projects fabricated.

- Go to the company web site.

- Visit the company's booth at a tradeshow, if possible.

- See if there are projects in your area the company has manufactured.

Of course, Hyla feels Fiberoptic Lighting, Inc., is the best company to fabricate fiber optic displays. She says the most important element in taking on a new project is integrity and knowing when to say "NO!"

With fiber optics, almost anything is possible. We like to say, "You dream...and we'll build!"

For information:

call (800) 543-2533 or e-mail hyla@cdsnet.net

www.fiberoptic-lighting.com

fli. ®

FIBEROPTIC○LIGHTING
I N C O R P O R A T E D

SUCCESS

Secret

#7

"Super" Tradeshow Transportation Strategies

by

United Van Lines, Inc.

"Super" Tradeshow Transportation Strategies

United Van Lines, Inc.

It's "Super Sunday." The host city has been bustling with pregame festivities for several days. Now it's game day. Thousands of fans prepare to fill the stadium for the Super Bowl.

However, something funny happens on the way to the kickoff. The favored team's star running back—possibly dreaming of an MVP performance—hits the snooze bar one too many times and misses the team bus from the hotel to the stadium. He catches a cab, but stadium gridlock causes further delay. He arrives at the players' entrance only to be detained by over-zealous security. Finally he arrives on the field, but has missed most of the pregame warm-ups. On his first carry, he pulls a muscle and is forced to sit out the rest of the game. His team goes on to lose the Super Bowl.

A stretch? Perhaps. But apply this analogy to a "Super Bowl" of tradeshows and one might not be entirely out of bounds.

Travel arrangements, exhibit designs and other pre-event festivities might transpire flawlessly. However, unless the "star players"—exhibit materials—arrive and depart in a timely and damage-free manner, the event will probably be a losing effort.

Of all the key players in a tradeshow, few have a more significant impact than transportation. Although transportation cost might constitute a relatively low percentage of your overall tradeshow budget, a breakdown in this area could lead to substantial losses in time and money. Therefore, when considering this important element, it is critical for exhibit managers to devise a game plan well in advance.

Create a Transportation Game Plan

When considering options to transport materials, exhibit managers have several choices—van line, common motor carrier, air freight, or company-owned vehicle. Although price likely is a consideration, it should not be the lone deciding factor. As an exhibit manager, you want a transportation company that approaches tradeshows as a full-time endeavor and a business priority. In that regard, it is best to select an established, respected van line to fill your transportation needs.

Experienced van line personnel understand the pressure a traffic manager is under at show time. They also understand the strict rules and regulations that govern trade show environments. Moreover, they have the resources, experience and industry knowledge to handle this important tradeshow element.

Go With a Pro

As a tradeshow approaches, exhibit management can become overwhelming. Placing the transportation responsibility in the hands of an experienced, specialized professional carrier affords exhibit managers at least some semblance of control.

How do you determine the best carrier for your needs? One telling sign is the presence within a transportation company of a separate department dedicated to handling tradeshows.

United Van Lines, for example, features a specialized exhibit department which dispatches and monitors each shipment by computer, facilitating on-time arrivals. The company further enhances dependability by offering a satellite communications and vehicle location system—in-van technology allowing United to pinpoint the location of tradeshow vans and communicate with van operators. Via this system, instructions about loading, order changes, and new order assignments can be sent directly to a terminal in the van's tractor.

In addition, the satellite system automatically tracks and updates the van's location every hour. Customers who have an Internet connection can access the information through the company's Web site.

At major shows, experienced United representatives are available on-site to assist customers and serve as liaisons with the drayage companies. The company also features a dedicated tradeshow fleet with experienced van operators. United drivers operate air-ride suspension vans which reduce the vibration of sensitive show materials. And if time is a critical factor, the company offers air service to any point in the world.

The following is a summary of tradeshow-specific features an organization should consider when choosing a service provider:

- Specialized exhibit/tradeshow department
- Satellite communications and vehicle location system
- Crated or pad-wrapped service
- Air-ride suspension fleet
- Climate-controlled vans
- On-site show representatives
- Dedicated, experienced trade show fleet staff

Review Your Strategy

When deciding on your carrier, consider the following points. If your carrier can provide positive answers to these questions, you are on the right road to determining a source for your display and exhibit transportation needs:

Guaranteed, consistent service

- Can your selected carrier provide evidence of considerable experience in exhibit and display transportation, as well as a list of satisfied customers?

Accessibility/customer service

- Does your selected carrier provide communications seven days a week, 24 hours a day?

- Is the carrier responsive to your changing needs?

- Does the carrier feature in-van technology, including a satellite vehicle tracking and communications system?

- Does the carrier include knowledgeable on-site representatives to assist customers and serve as liaisons with drayage companies?

Proper equipment and protection to handle your exhibit

- Does your carrier's equipment have air-ride suspension to reduce the vibration of sensitive show material?

- Is each trailer equipped with pads, logistics straps, decking, dollies, and other devices to meet the requirements for your specific shipment?

- Does the driver know how to use the equipment?

- Are the vehicles clean and in good repair?

Capabilities

- Can the carrier handle uncrated, pad-wrapped exhibits for direct show delivery?

- Can the carrier handle crated, less-than-truckload (LTL) and truckload shipments either to tender to a drayage contractor or for direct delivery?

- Do shipments go direct on the same vehicle with no setoffs or transfers to other trucks?

Professionalism

- Does the salesperson show a genuine interest in you and your business, with a noticeable readiness to help ease your workload?

- Are the drivers neat, knowledgeable and skillful in their handling of your exhibit?

- Does the carrier have the capability and the willingness to help if an emergency arises?

- Is the carrier really oriented toward exhibit transportation?

Reputation

- Does the carrier participate in any large shows in an "official carrier" capacity?

- What is the carrier's reputation among drayage companies for promptness and cooperation?

- Do the drivers know the loading and unloading requirements and understand the physical layouts of major show facilities around the country?

Make a Victorious Exit

You and your staff have spent months preparing for the show, and the hard work has paid off. Your exhibit was a success. However, one more important item remains on your to-do list—the "move-out" of your exhibit.

The following step-by-step instructions should help facilitate this final, critical phase of the tradeshow. By following these points, you can assist in getting your exhibit off the show floor and on its way to the next destination:

- Prior to the finish of the show, determine your booth shipping requirements.

- Thoroughly review move-out information that is circulated by show management and/or the drayage contractor. This will alert you to the sequence of events that will take place, such as when to expect empty containers or how to obtain authorization to hand-carry certain items from the exhibit hall.

- In order for the drayage contractor to remove the exhibit or product from your booth and have it available for the carrier to load, authorization must be given to the drayage contractor. This is accomplished by completing the drayage contractor's Short Form Bill of Lading (shipping order).

- The Short Form Bill of Lading is available only from the drayage contractor at the freight desk, which usually is located in the service area of the exhibit hall. This document must be completed as instructed by the drayage contractor.

- If your exhibit or product is being shipped to more than one consignee or delivery address, a separate Short Form Bill of Lading must be completed for each destination, even when the exhibit is loaded on the same truck.

- If your exhibit requires multiple trucks consigned to one address, a Short Form Bill of Lading should be completed and turned in for each truck. When a piece count is known, indicate the number on the truck's Bill of Lading. When the count is unknown, mark the first truck's Bill of Lading with the total piece count and subsequent bills with the words "overflow truck."

- After your exhibit is packed, label all pieces, indicating the exact delivery address. After completing the Short Form Bill of Lading, promptly return it to the freight desk so that the driver can get in line. When an installation and dismantling company turns in the Short Form Bill of Lading, be certain that the firm has your instructions to name the carrier.

- The driver will report to the drayage contractor's freight desk with the Bill of Lading, requesting to load your booth. The drayage contractor verifies your carrier selection as noted on the Short Form Bill of Lading, and the driver is assigned a dock to load. When a carrier is not named, the drayage contractor reserves the right to name one.

Talkin' the Talk

As with any area of business, the exhibit/tradeshow industry has a language all its own. Here are some commonly used terms and definitions that you'll find helpful in understanding the requirements to be a part of "show" business:

Association

An organized body of people who sponsor a show. They may manage the show using their executive staff, designate a membership committee to manage it, or hire an outside show management firm.

Direct Delivery

Transportation of your exhibit from origin to the exhibit hall, rather than from origin to a drayage warehouse. Direct delivery provides more time to prepare your exhibit and reduces the chance for damage resulting from multiple handling. Direct delivery is routinely offered by van lines. Common carriers usually do not provide this service.

Drayage

The movement of exhibits within the exhibit hall, including storage of empty crates and cartons. Drayage normally is handled by an official drayage contractor which is responsible for maintaining "in" and "out" traffic schedules for the loading dock and freight doors. The drayage contractor usually can receive your crated freight at a warehouse prior to the show and deliver it on the target date. Drayage details are explained in the exhibitor's manual provided by show management.

Exhibitor's Manual

A document published and distributed by show management which sets forth the basic information and regulations by which the show will operate. The exhibitor must fully and carefully read the manual and share it with everyone assisting in the exhibit, including vendors. Contact your carrier's representative to review the shipping/drayage section.

Freight Desk

The drayage contractor's desk in the exhibit hall. All Bills of Lading must be submitted here. The desk usually is located in the service area.

Hard Card

Usually the hard back copy of the Short Form Bill of Lading. When a carrier checks in at the freight desk, the drayage contractor processes the document and returns the hard card. The carrier must have this to line up for loading.

Pad Wrap

A special service through which exhibits are wrapped in protective quilted cloth rather than being crated. Pad wrapping saves the cost of crate-building and offers exhibit-building design flexibilities. Pads should remain on the exhibit until it has reached the floor booth space, and the exhibit should be rewrapped on the show floor before move-out begins. Pad wrap service is available only from van lines and a few specialty carriers.

Short Form Bill of Lading

An abbreviated shipping document prepared for all outbound shipments and presented to the freight desk. The Bill of Lading must specify the number of pieces to be moved and the name of the carrier handling the shipment. If no carrier is named, one will be assigned by the drayage company. It is your responsibility to pick up the form at the freight desk, complete it and turn it in.

Show Management

The organization responsible for all aspects of the tradeshow. It selects the location and facility, sells the exhibit space, chooses official contractors, and makes and enforces the show's rules and regulations.

Target Date

A specified date on which the exhibit must arrive at the exhibit hall. Occasionally, a time also is specified. If the shipment is checked in on time at the freight desk, the drayage contractor will see that it unloads on schedule. Missed target dates/times may result in higher drayage charges.

Weight Ticket

A small piece of paper on which weight has been stamped at a truck scale. Every tradeshow exhibit must have weight tickets, which are the carrier's responsibility. There are absolutely no exceptions. Drayage charges are based on the weight specified on the carrier's Bill of Lading, unless the actual weight is verified.

Carefully selecting the best way for your organization to ship tradeshow materials will assure your team the opportunity to win at tradeshow exhibiting.

United Van Lines, Inc.

From its relatively humble beginnings in the 1920s, United Van Lines has grown into a worldwide total transportation and relocation services company routinely handling the most complex shipments safely and on time. In addition to being the nation's largest household goods mover, the suburban St. Louis-based company also specializes in the worldwide movement of tradeshow exhibits, electronics/high-value products and other specialized commodities.

Although many carriers offer tradeshow/exhibit moving service, the real test is being able to deliver the same level of dependability—show after show, year after year. United has been providing specialized transportation service since 1959 when the company developed its exclusive *Safe-Guard* service for special handling.

Each year, United and its agents load and deliver more than 160,000 tradeshow and special commodities shipments. The company's specialized exhibit department dispatches and monitors each shipment by computer to ensure on-schedule arrivals. Service dependability is further enhanced by United's *VanStar* satellite tracking and communications system—in-van technology that allows the company to pinpoint the location of tradeshow vans and communicate with van operators.

At major shows, experienced United representatives are available on-site to assist customers and serve as liaisons with the drayage companies. Exhibit managers also can depend on a dedicated group of tradeshow drivers who take pride in protecting exhibits from origin to final destination. United drivers rely on air-ride vans, which reduce the vibration of sensitive show material. And if time is critical for an exhibit delivery, United offers air service to any point in the world.

United Van Lines maintains a nationwide network of 500 affiliated agencies, with 500 additional representatives in 135 other countries throughout the world. Ask a local United agent for more information about the company's tradeshow/exhibit capabilities. Additional information about United Van Lines and its services can be obtained through United's Web site at *www.unitedvanlines.com*.

SUCCESS

Secret #8

How to Run a Successful Pre-show Meeting

by
Susan A. Friedmann

How to Run a Successful Pre-show Meeting

Susan A. Friedmann

Pre-show meetings should be organized, informative, and fun. However, the typical meeting is often very humdrum, a matter-of-fact recitation of new product information or basic exhibiting logistics. In short, most pre-show meetings are *boring*.

This is not the way to get your team fired-up and enthused about the upcoming time on the show floor. When meetings like this are perceived as being time-wasters, it's difficult to motivate your team. What's missing is some excitement. Just like a major sports team getting ready to play its best game of the season, your people need motivation. Working a show is hard work and is often a case of "survival of the fittest." Frequently you and your team need to be "ON" for 12 to 18 hours a day, for three or more days at a stretch. Staying motivated is often a real challenge, especially at the end of a day or during the final hours of the show when traffic is usually slow, time seems to stand still, and your feet hurt.

The energy, motivation and stamina your team needs to stay revved up for the duration of the show comes in three different forms: *personal motivation, manager inspiration,* and *team spirit.* It is critical to understand each of these different areas to better understand how to incorporate them into your program.

Personal Motivation. The key ingredient for anyone to be motivated to work a show is simple: *they need to want to be there.* Too often, employees are told by management to "just show up" to work a particular show. However, given a choice, they would often prefer not to. Sales people frequently feel it interferes with their normal selling routine. When employees have a negative attitude about being at a show, their body language lets everyone around know how they feel—that this is a futile and unimportant exercise.

It is important to remember that everyone representing your company is an ambassador. By being helpful, courteous and having a professional demeanor, they can strengthen the company's image and gain new customers. Therefore, they should be carefully chosen based on their excellent knowledge of the company's products/services and their ability to interface with the many customers and prospects expected to visit the exhibit.

Manager Inspiration. One of the major reasons booth staff have a negative attitude about being at a show comes about when upper management's negative feelings filter down. The reverse also applies. When top management is supportive of the company's tradeshow activities and demonstrates their feelings by attending the show, helping in the booth, taking part in training programs and pre- and post-show activities, the enthusiasm is contagious.

It is management's responsibility to create a positive, fun and reinforcing environment and to realize that it takes more than company goals to succeed. Rewards and personal recognition provide an effective way of encouraging higher levels of performance. A range of tools, from personal thank you's to a variety of rewards, are useful ways to recognize accomplishments, such as exhibiting goals achieved, new orders, quality qualified leads, etc. One company gave away three Mont Blanc pens every day of the show to the best booth staffers. Competition was high and many staff members started making recommendations for winners based on their own observations.

Team Spirit. Everyone in the booth should be working together as a team, helping each other out whenever and wherever necessary. If there is a large number of staffers, split them into teams with technical people working alongside sales people. Encourage them to establish plans of action for working the show and promote a certain amount of autonomy within the groups. Managers need to create an environment of camaraderie where the staff, as a team, will want to pull out all the stops to succeed and set themselves apart from the competition.

Team members should be persuaded to coach their colleagues, for example, by pointing out negative non-verbal behavior. Managers can also create games to foster competitiveness among the teams. You can use your review sessions after each day to recognize superlative performance. In addition, this is an opportunity to encourage team members to give and receive feedback from their colleagues. The purpose is to look for ways to improve past performance and make each day better than the previous one. Managers need to remember that individual achievement is worth group recognition.

Before the Show

A pep rally before the show will get your team fired up and remind them of what it takes to perform successfully. A key component to having exciting, effective pre-show meetings is to make it relevant and fun.

When and Where

Most pre-show meetings should take place within a week or two prior to the event. Any sooner and the momentum (and information) is forgotten; any later and participants will be too distracted by last-minute preparations.

If possible, the meeting should held away from the company. This separates people from the distractions of phones, being paged, and people hovering around their desk or cubicle. If meeting off-site is not feasible, consider having the meeting before or after business hours, in order to limit distractions.

How-To

The following 10 guidelines will help you create a meeting that gets your team fired-up and enthused about the upcoming time on the show floor:

1. Develop a plan

Include your meeting as part of your overall exhibit program. Map out exactly what you want to cover, how much time you need, who needs to be involved, and the best time and location for the meeting to be held. Plan on covering the following four essential key areas:

Why your company is exhibiting.

What your company is exhibiting.

What you expect from your team.

How to do what is expected.

You will also probably want to include short discussions on lead generation and retrieval, handling the media, and meeting with large customers or prospects.

Why your company is exhibiting

It is vital for everyone to fully understand the purpose of your organization's involvement in the show and what you are expecting to achieve by participating. Goals need to be quantifiable, such as generating 250 quality leads or selling $250,000 of products/services. This is the only way you will be able to measure your level of success.

What your company is exhibiting

To avoid any surprises, let your team know which specific products/services are going to be exhibited. This is particularly true for just-released products or those that have not been on the market for very long. I often come across staff members who know nothing about the products being displayed and feel totally inadequate at the booth. No one bothered to check their particular product knowledge or trained them on the new items. Last-minute training is often not adequate. Remember that your people are your ambassadors and represent everything your company stands for. If they are unfamiliar with what is being exhibited, it conveys a negative impression of your company to the prospect.

What you expect from your team

Your team needs to be encouraged to set its own goals based on the overall exhibiting goals. They also need to know what you want them to be doing on a daily basis. For example, how many people do you expect them to interact with and what kind of information do you want? Empower your team to do what it takes to help visitors.

How to do what is expected

Using a knowledgeable staff member or an outside consultant, train your representatives to be more effective on the show floor. Show them how to demonstrate the products on display and qualify prospects effectively. Allow time to practice during your meetings. With my clients, I often conduct role-play scenarios/warm-up sessions, which give participants a chance to practice the necessary skills in a safe environment.

2. Consider timing

At the pre-show meeting, provide clear information (preferably in a written format) regarding exhibit dates and times, travel requirements, and any other meeting-related appointments or requirements (such as any pre-arranged company hospitality). Travel dates in particular need to be spelled out. For example, if the show starts on a Wednesday and set-up is the day before, on Tuesday, it would not be good if all staff members flew in Tuesday afternoon or evening.

The distance traveled, possible jet lag from time changes, and the size and complexity of the city where the show is taking place will help determine and set timing parameters regarding arrival, attendance during the show, and departure.

3. Make it mandatory

Often your tradeshow veterans consider it unnecessary to attend pre-show meetings because of a "been there, done that" attitude. They believe that they won't learn anything new and that the meeting is a waste of time, so they opt not to attend. However, if you want to create a cohesive team, everyone needs to be there. This is particularly true if your organization is launching or announcing a new product, or if your organization has several newcomers who do not have extensive show experience.

To convince tradeshow veterans to attend, consider using their expertise by involving them in the program. Topics for them to cover include key customers or prospects to watch for, lessons learned from previously attending this show, and particular greetings, questions or product demonstration methods that have worked well in the past.

Another benefit to having everyone attend a pre-show meeting is that it builds teamwork, which may not come naturally. Your pre-show meetings help create a unified team, which *increases productivity, raises the level of professionalism and improves attitudes about working the show.* During the meeting, encourage formal and informal interaction to open up the lines of communication and develop a greater team cohesiveness. Allow time for your team to get to know each other better, discuss issues, concerns, etc. Your people are often so busy doing their thing in the field that they don't take any time for reflection, learning and dialogue with their colleagues. However, their discussion time should be structured so that the meeting isn't sidetracked or bogged down with unnecessary issues.

4. Encourage top management's support

Making top management an integral part of your exhibit team creates a totally different attitude within the group. When top management cares about what happens at the show, team members quickly realize the seriousness of the company's investment, which results in a more focused and committed group effort.

The following are ways to encourage top management's support:

- Have them kick the meeting off with a few words in support of the company's tradeshow investment.

- Use their expertise and have them address a specific topic during the program.

- Consider asking them how they would like to be involved.

5. *Plan on having fun*

Think of your meeting as a pep rally rather than a boring humdrum meeting. Again, just like a major sports team getting ready to play its biggest game of the season, your people need motivation. Instead of calling it a pre-show meeting, consider having a team appreciation party or have a theme event. Motivating your people to attend is the first stage. They are more likely to attend if they feel it'll be fun and, of course, worthwhile.

Ways to have fun and stimulate participants at pre-show meetings include:

- Use game show techniques.
- Form teams and have competitive exercises.
- Conduct problem-solving exercises.
- Organize a quiz after each presentation.
- Have plenty of prizes for participation.

When done properly, your pre-show meetings will turn into events people *want* to attend.

6. *Choose carefully who will run the meeting*

The person who conducts the meeting usually makes or breaks its effectiveness. Have someone who is knowledgeable and motivating. If you have people within the organization who are good speakers, animated and inspiring, use them. Make sure that they are well respected and that your staff will listen to them and follow their advice. Age and expertise are often important factors.

Here are ways to help the meeting leader or facilitator run a great meeting:

- Require the meeting to have an agenda and that the meeting leader stick to it. Nothing bogs down a meeting than one or more people discussing non-pertinent topics.

- Establish a set length of time at the beginning and have the meeting leader stick to it. If participants know that a meeting will last a certain length of time, they will be more likely to concentrate during the entire session. People become bored or lose their train of thought when meetings drag on endlessly.

- Vary who runs the meetings. If you exhibit at several shows during the course of a year, consider varying who leads the pre-show meeting to keep freshness, variety and spontaneity.

7. *Consider outside resources*

Hiring an outside consultant or speaker to help generate show motivation often brings a fresh set of ideas to the group. In addition, information coming from an outside expert is usually viewed more positively than when delivered by internal personnel. Consider using your own people for product/company information and outside resources for overall show etiquette.

Visual aids help people concentrate better and remember much more. When I conduct pre-show programs for my clients, I always show slides of scenes I have taken on the show floor depicting many of the dos and don'ts of professional booth behavior. These pictures paint a picture worth a thousand words and the images stay in people's minds for at least the duration of the show, if not longer.

8. *Reinforce booth behavior*

Make sure that everyone understands that they are company ambassadors. By being helpful, courteous and having a professional demeanor, they can strengthen the company's image and gain new customers. Tradeshow research states that 85% of the visitor's impression about your exhibit is determined by your staff's attitude and behavior, and 80% of a final buying decision can be influenced by the booth interaction.

Specific areas to cover include:

- Dress and appearance (include dress code specifics)
- Appropriate greetings
- Qualifying questions
- Acceptable and unacceptable booth etiquette
- Lead capturing information
- Arrangements for media visits (specify company spokespeople)
- Meal arrangements during and after the show
- Transportation issues to and from the show

9. Encourage goal setting

Encourage each team member to set a personal goal for the show. This helps to increase their accountability, and also builds motivation. At the pre-show meeting have everyone share their goal with a colleague, and then at post-show or debriefing meetings, encourage them to report on their successes.

10. Create an incentive program

Rewards and personal recognition provide an effective way of encouraging higher levels of performance. Creating an incentive program for your team to recognize accomplishments, such as exhibiting goals achieved, new orders, quality qualified leads, etc., is an important way to stimulate enthusiasm and accountability.

Managers need to know their individual team members and what motivates them. Studies show that more people are motivated by personal recognition and appreciation than by money. Have a plan as to how you will recognize and reward good behavior and performance, such as having a MVBP (Most Value Booth Person) for each day.

Summary

The usefulness of your pre-show meeting comes specifically from offering your team pertinent information, clearly communicated. Don't let your meeting run out of steam. Keep your participants stimulated and focused and the energy of the meeting high. Have an agenda that includes breaks, movement, visual aids, toys, group discussion and music. Group discussion is often key as many companies use their pre-show meetings as an opportunity for the sales team to get together.

As you think about how best to inspire boundless enthusiasm and encourage staff to have a winning attitude on the show floor, remember that motivation moves people and the power of recognition can fire up personal productivity. Whatever you do, make it fun and effective and success will surely follow.

Susan A. Friedmann

Susan works with organizations that want to attract new business at tradeshows and with show organizers and exhibitors who want to retain and grow their customer base.

She works one-on-one or with teams to help boost tradeshow results. She also conducts presentations and workshops for groups nationally and internationally. She provides her clients with what they need to know to attract more business by focusing on four critical areas: planning, promotion, people and productivity. She identifies and helps people develop certain skills that are critical to their trade show success now and in the future. She shows people how to build better relationships with customers, prospects and advocates in the marketplace to retain and grow their business.

Originally from London, England, Susan has been a coach, speaker and author for over 20 years. Her extensive experience in the tradeshow industry has allowed her to work with several hundred companies representing more than 30 different industries in the U.S. and in Europe.

As an innovative and insightful speaker, Susan has been featured at major conventions and in the media. An abridged version of her book *Exhibiting at Trade Shows: Tips and Techniques for Success* has been translated into French, German, Italian and Spanish. In addition, she is a regular contributing editor to numerous professional and trade publications, in particular, *Convene, Cintermex, Ideas, Exhibitor Times, and Exhibitor Marketing Magazine.* Most recently, she compiled and published the latest books on exhibiting, *Secrets of Successful Exhibiting* series.

To find out how Susan Friedmann, The Tradeshow Coach can help your tradeshow success, call (518) 523-1320.

Exhibit Marketing Systems that Work

The Nuts & Bolts of Selling at Tradeshows
This dynamic *"how-to"* video is packed full of practical, easy-to-use information that guarantees every exhibitor more successful and profitable results from tradeshows. Watch as Susan Friedmann reveals techniques to:

- *Help you identify and approach interested prospects*
- *Provide a formula for qualifying prospects to obtain quality information for future follow-up*
- *Give you specific steps to take charge of the conversation that creates and maintains a high quality image*
- *Help you develop effective listening techniques that make every prospect feel important*
- *Eliminate spending unnecessary time with uninterested parties*
- *Communicate professional closing techniques that outline future follow-up action.*

Once you have discovered Susan's new ideas, and mastered her latest proven techniques and special skills, you will see an instant return on your tradeshow investment!

VHS Video Cassette (20 min.)　　　*(PAL version available)*
　　　　　　　　　　　　　　　　Regular price:　$199

Exhibiting at Tradeshows: Tips & Techniques for Success
An easy read for the beginner and a good reminder for the pro. It contains numerous easy-to-use and practical *"how-to"* strategies for successful and profitable exhibiting results. Whether you are a one-person operation or a multinational corporation, exhibit at a trade show or consumer show, a conference, exposition, or mall show, there is something in here for you. *This book is a required survival kit for every exhibitor!*

Softcover Book (Customization available)　　*Regular price:　$15*

Secrets of Successful Exhibiting Series
From some of America's leading tradeshow professionals, these books share useful, practical information to help make every exhibiting experience pay off—no matter what size the show, or exhibit. Offering sound professional advice and guidance—a formula for success to master the unique, high-pressure exhibiting environment. Packed with a wealth of success strategies, tips and insights, you will find answers to many of your exhibiting questions. *3 Softcover Books*　　　　*One book:　$19.95*
　　　　　　　　　　　　　　　Set of two books:　$35.00
　　　　　　　　　　　　　　　Set of three books:　$45.00

ExhibiTips—The Collection

This 48-page loose-leaf manual is a collection of hundreds of practical tips and techniques on all aspects of tradeshow exhibiting from Exhibit Management through Boothmanship, Sales & Marketing, International Exhibiting and Professional Development. Learn the do's & don'ts of successful tradeshow exhibiting from marketing before the event, through working with labor unions at the show, greeting & qualifying prospects, proper exhibitor behavior, and follow-up strategies that you put in place before your prospect even leaves the show.

Loose-leaf Manual (48 pages)　　　　　　　*Regular price: $50*

ExhibitSmart series –

7 Steps to Exhibiting Success • 101 Cost-Cutting Tips for the Savvy Exhibitor • 62 Powerful Questions to Qualify Your Prospects • 10 Steps to Making Your Show Leads Pay Off

Each booklets presents cutting-edge, proven techniques that improve skills, increase confidence and get results. Perfect for those who want practical, easy-to-apply methods that will help them create a competitive edge at every show.

Regular price: $6.95 each, the four-book set is $25

7 Steps to Exhibiting Success

This powerful audio cassette tape and booklet guides you through the simple SUCCESS formula every exhibitor needs to make a difference and get results on the show floor.

Regular price: $24.95

Unconditional 100% Money-back Guarantee Order

Call: 800-647-5455
Fax: 518-523-8755

S U S A N   F R I E D M A N N
THE
TRADESHOW COACH

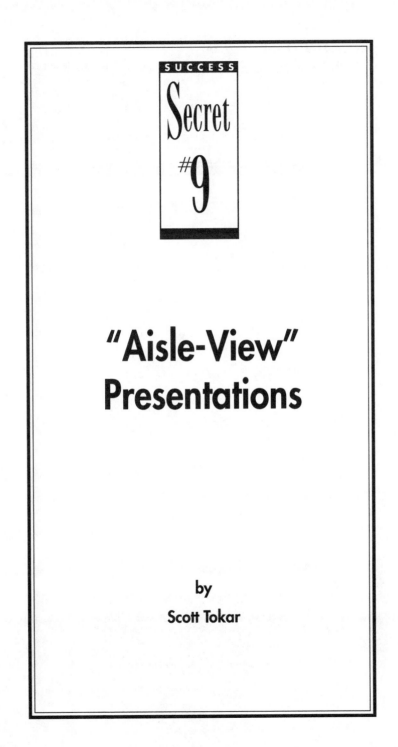

SUCCESS

Secret #9

"Aisle-View" Presentations

by
Scott Tokar

"Aisle-View" Presentations

Scott Tokar

*"You weren't kidding when you said you
wanted to break our goal of 300 leads for
the show—we were stunned when we walked
out the first day with 308!! It was agreed
that your delivery of our message and
product offerings was more clear, persuasive,
and memorable than many of our multimedia theater presentations utilized in our
large corporate booth."*
— Jennifer Condren, Trade Show Manager,
Banyan Systems.

Walk down any trade show aisle and you'll quickly
discover that many exhibitors have gone way beyond
the traditional trade show marketing approach. The
scope and style of trade show selling has changed dra-
matically in the last few years. Come to think of it,
just about every aspect of advertising and marketing
has changed as well... The growing popularity of the
Internet and MTV has made information more visual
and message delivery even more rapid than before.

This new emphasis on "faster and more visual" is
why more and more exhibitors are discovering that the
average corporate booth structure, graphics, and brochures don't seem to be attracting the attention or leads
they once did. Not only is something extra needed to make
visitors stop, the attendee must be "visually" educated
on the features and benefits of the product and then be
directed to the proper sales person for more detailed information. In study after study* and through direct

---

*See report #5040 from The Trade Show Bureau, Colorado

company testimonial, the exhibiting industry has discovered the advantages of professional live presentations.

The typical "Theater-Style" presentation is a perfect solution for a large exhibit on the trade show floor. These exhibits incorporate a mini-theater complete with an elevated stage area, lighting, sound, and a dozen or so chairs. In many cases the theater area will take up fifty percent or more of a larger 50'x50' exhibit space. The audience response and crowd draw to this style of marketing is phenomenal.

But, what if your company has a *smaller* booth? What if you are attending a show that caters to a secondary market, or if you don't have the budget for a full "theater style" production? How can you obtain the same impact for *your* exhibit as the 50x50 island exhibits at the front entrance of the trade show hall? The answer: An "Aisle-View" presentation.

What is an "Aisle-View" presentation?

An "Aisle-View" presentation is a form of live presenting that draws a large crowd directly from a trade show aisle. Normal crowds can range from 20 to 50 attendees while at the largest of trade shows it's not uncommon to see crowds of 80 to 100 or more attending a single presentation. The "Aisle-View" presentation requires only 3'x3' of valuable exhibit space, there is no need for chairs, and the performance surface is usually a pre-existing podium or table that matches your exhibit. If you are a regular to the trade show marketplace, you have probably seen one of these live presentations in action: Magicians, jugglers, mimes, caricature artists, models, or robots. All of these attractions will stop traffic and generate large crowds. To be completely successful, however, you'll also need to educate the attendees as well as generate measurable leads for your sales team.

For example, a mime may catch the attendees' attention for a few minutes, but it's difficult to get a serious marketing message across if the presenter can't answer any questions. And, some of the "Aisle-View" techniques have a limit on the maximum number of attendees that they can stop, such as a caricature artist. A robot may be able to recite your company's sales slogan, but how will you obtain the follow-up information and qualify the leads?

The secret is to develop an "Aisle-View" presentation that will stop large crowds, deliver a corporate message without looking like a carnival or a sideshow, and have a built-in lead capture technique to follow-up with the hot prospects as well as aide in measuring the attraction's results after the show.

Trade Show Magic

Trade show magic has a wonderful advantage over other techniques in the "Aisle-View" category. Just look at the multi-BILLION dollar casinos in Las Vegas: they learned long ago that magic builds crowds—BIG crowds. Since 1989, the magician team of Siegfried & Roy has been attracting sold-out crowds to the Mirage Hotel. Why? Simply because magic has an incredibly wide appeal; everyone likes to be amazed no matter what their industry or occupation. What's more, in today's politically correct corporate climate, magic doesn't rely on scantily clad models or "booth-babes" to attract attention. If a trade show magician is a true professional, it's often difficult to tell him/her apart from a booth's sales staff (except for the microphone and the large crowds). The magical presenter will typically speak with authority, using the right buzz words and acronyms. If the sales staff is in a booth uniform, or a three-piece suit, the presenter will usually match them as well. This helps to blur the line between magician and sales staff, and it allows the exhibitor's message to be taken more seriously.

There's usually one problem, however: Magic looks like fun, which confuses (or even alarms!) most in the corporate world. Many wonder: Can you really mix a serious corporate message into a humorous and amazing demonstration? You bet! Magic is a unique, mind-active form of entertainment. Can you remember the last time you saw a magician? Do you remember thinking to yourself, "How did he do that"? The key here is that you were *thinking*—your mind was working, awake, and you were paying attention! It's at this very moment that a professional "Aisle-View" magician adds the commercial message. The audience can't forget the message because their mind was active and alert the entire time! It's all in the timing, which most professional magicians have mastered.

The Message

As with any live presentation, you'll want to make sure that the right message is being delivered to the maximum number of attendees. A professional trade show magician will make sure that your message is the number one priority and that the magic tricks are secondary. Try to think of an "Aisle-View" presentation the same way you would look at a promotional video for your company. The TV and the video tape player are just vehicles to deliver the content, your message, to the audience; the program that is playing on the TV is your prime concern. Any presentation method you can think of is simply a vehicle, the TV, for your message. Of course, some TV programs are more interesting than others, and they are more likely to catch your attention and keep you watching longer than the boring ones. Obviously, more people are likely to stop and watch HBO than C-SPAN, so don't discount the delivery, but the corporate message needs to shine through first.

A professional live presentation firm will always provide the exhibitor with a script, or at the very least an outline, of the presentation. A typical "Aisle-View" script will clearly explain the actions of your presenter as well as your message incorporation. Sometimes this will be a quick outline of a magic trick and then an example of how this action fits with a particular message. Or, you may end up with more of a line-by-line "script." Either example is fine, as long as the exhibitor has the opportunity to review the message and make any clarifications or changes to the content.

Most live presentation firms will have a standard way to collect this scripting information for the writing process. The key here is to boil down the company's complex marketing material into a clear and concise message that can be easily understood by the masses. With the large crowd draw at your booth you'll be attracting some hot leads, as well as several good prospects, and many looky-loos. Your message needs to attract those hot leads and the prospects. However, you'll also need to make your message clear enough so that the looky-loos won't waste your sales staff's time trying to figure out what you are selling. You'll need a way to spark the interest in the right attendees so that they will ask more detailed questions and identify themselves to your sales staff for a sales call or a follow-up.

An "Aisle-View" presentation is inherently more open and interactive than a regular sit-down "Theater-Style" show. Why? It's very rare that your performer will stick to a word-for-word script because the presentation is taking place on the aisle, reducing the barriers for the audience to ask questions and react to the presentation. Just make sure that your presenter is familiar enough with your products and your message to confidently add off-the-cuff remarks at random to the presentation. Most "Aisle-View" presenters will ask for product brochures, corporate profiles, and web site links to help them learn more about a company. This research, though time consuming, is the key to blurring the line between your performer and the sales staff.

A good presenter will always try to incorporate what is called a "salivating statement" during the presentation. This is a statement that whets the appetite of your potential customers, forcing them to ask for more detailed information from your sales staff. Sometimes an exhibitor's best advertising can sound like a wild claim. This will demand clarification by the sales staff, but only from your *targeted* customers. For instance, "Did you know that Doohicky Inc. just broke all speed records in the Widget category, and at half the cost of other Widget manufacturers? How? Ask our sales staff for the results of the latest independent study." This kind of statement may sound impossible to current or potential Widget users in the crowd and they'll demand further explanation. They'll want to see proof of the independent study. That's great! This kind of statement increases your sales staff's one-on-one effectiveness and opens a line of communication with the right attendees. In this example, only current (or potential) Widget users will want to know more. However, the same statement educated the looky-loos, telling them what the company is all about. Their curiosity is satisfied and as a member of your crowd they'll have helped you to add the right "buzz" to the trade show floor.

"Buzz"

Have you ever been to a trade show where everyone is talking about a particular booth? Several aisles away you can hear people telling their friends and colleges about the exhibit that they just can't miss. Attendees chat about these companies while in a hotel elevator or at the reception after the trade show floor is closed. This is called "Buzz." Buzz is wonderful: it's free advertising, helping you repeat your sales message even when you aren't there. Buzz also helps your exhibit sell long after a trade show is over as people are more apt to remember your organization—and of course its products. Wouldn't you like to be the booth creating that buzz? Of course!

Every visitor to an "Aisle-View" presentation helps feed the buzz on the trade show floor, whether they are your target customers or not. In fact, non-customers generate most of the buzz outside the exhibit hall. These looky-loos are the people that have probably never heard your company's message. So, not only is the "Aisle-View" presentation new to them, your features and benefits are as well. These non-customers will be talking to your target prospects in seminars and while they are waiting for the convention center bus. Therefore, a looky-loo is a critical component to the "Aisle-View" buzz.

It's simple to tell whether your booth is creating the right "buzz" or not. If you hear someone on a trade show floor say, "Wow, that magician two aisles over is great," you DO NOT have the right buzz. On the other hand, if you hear someone say: "Wow, you've gotta go see that magician at the Doohickey booth!" you've done it! What's the difference? Name recognition. **If the attendees are talking about the presentation but not the company name, your presentation has failed**. You must generate name recall to make the "buzz" pay off.

"Buzz" will also help your booth pull larger and larger crowds as each exhibit day goes on. Remember, the more potential customers your booth can attract, the more successful your presentation will be. In most shows you have a percentage of the attendees that are your exhibit's target prospect. Let's say that only ten percent of the visitors to any given show were your potential customers. If you could attract ten attendees per hour you should create one good lead for each hour. On the other hand, if you could attract 100 attendees per hour, you should end up with ten good leads per hour. That's a far better return on your exhibiting investment dollars. There is a small catch, however. In the first example you only had to sort through ten visitors to find the one good lead, while with the second example you had to weed through 100 attendees to get to the ten good prospects. This can make a big difference in the cost and time of post-show follow up. Hence, you will need an accurate way to qualify the increased leads an "Aisle-View" presentation can deliver.

Lead Capture

Big crowds! With a professional "Aisle-View" presentation you'll be generating huge crowds and, if your presenter is good, the leads are sure to follow. But you will need a way to sort through these leads. For some exhibitors a business card or a scan of an attendee's badge is enough to tell them if the visitor is a potential prospect or not. Sometimes you can tell just by the name of the visitor's company or their job title whether you should send them follow up information or not. But not all exhibitors are that lucky; they need more information to help them qualify a lead.

You can ask for this detailed qualifying information if you are willing to reward the visitor for their time. A T-shirt, a ball cap, or a free sample of your product is the perfect "bribe" for this knowledge. After the presentation, on a 3x5 card, ask for a visitor's contact information. Then, ask three yes or no, multiple choice, or true/false questions. This helps your staff determine the level of interest for each attendee. And since most people won't take the time to answer a fill in the blank questionnaire on a busy trade show floor, this makes it easy on your organization and the visitor. The three questions could be as basic as the following:

"Are you currently using our product?"

"Do you see a potential need at your organization for our products or services?"

"Would you like to talk with someone about your needs?"

As an incentive, you can give a premium to everyone that fills out a card or you can draw one card per presentation to select a winner. It's all up to you and your budget as to what reward, and how many of them, you would like to give away.

The Bottom Line

The most significant advantage of "Aisle-View" presentations is their low cost. Because an "Aisle-View" presentation takes up so little space in a booth, your exhibit space will cost less. And because your exhibit structure won't require a custom built stage or seating area, you'll be saving money with the exhibit builder too. And, due to the fact that most "Aisle-View" presentations use only one presenter, you'll save money on their travel expenses as well.

With no need of an expensive support staff for lights, sound and video, you'll quickly discover what many in the exhibit industry found out long ago—that an "Aisle-View" presentation is the ideal way to draw crowds to your booth, create a "buzz" around your organization, capture qualified leads, and help a smaller booth stand out from the crowd in the competitive world of live trade show marketing.

Scott Tokar

Scott Tokar is a magician and founder of Corporate-FX®. Having started his "Infotainment" career in 1984, he has helped scores of companies explain the features and benefits of their products using "Theater-Style" and "Aisle-View" magic as a communications medium. Over time, as Scott's reputation began to grow, the demand for his trade show magic became overwhelming. Even though he was an accomplished magician, he still couldn't master the trick of being in two places at one time. So Scott expanded in 1991, creating a team of skilled Infotainers, product presenters, and corporate magicians.

Scott's interest in magic began at the age of seven, when he was given a magic set as a present. By the age of 16, Scott had become a member of The Magic Castle's Junior Program for advanced and promising young magicians, and at age 20 he received the coveted Junior Achievement Award from the Castle's Board of Directors. To this day, Scott is ranked as one of the youngest members ever to receive this award.

In 1988, Scott won first place for Close-Up/Sleight of Hand Magic at the International Brotherhood of Magicians convention, and in 1991 he was nominated in the category of "Best Event Entertainment Concept" by caterers and event planners at their national convention sponsored by Special Event's Magazine.

Since that time, Scott has focused his attention exclusively on the corporate environment, producing live magic presentations for exhibitors at trade shows and in sales meetings around the world. In 1992, Scott received the "Best of Show" award while working for Downing Displays at the Exhibitor Show (a trade show about trade shows). He did it again in 1998 at the Fall Conference of the Exhibitor Show in Baltimore.

Today, the Corporate-FX® team continues to grow, and Scott Tokar is recognized as an industry expert in the field of live trade show marketing, infotainment, and of course his first love...the art of magic.

Call Toll-Free: 1.800.MAGIC.13

http:///www.CorporateFX.com

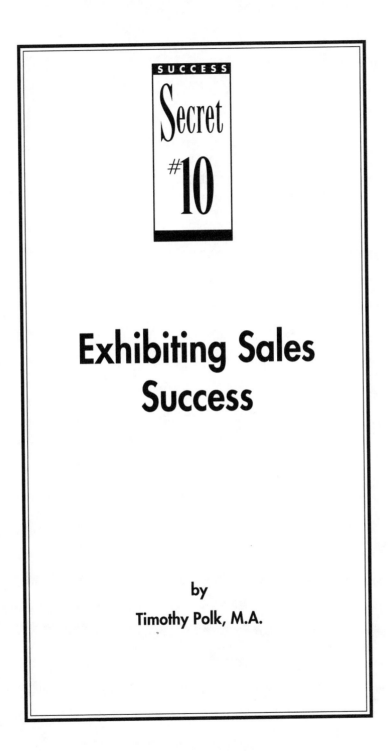

SUCCESS

Secret #10

Exhibiting Sales Success

by
Timothy Polk, M.A.

Exhibiting Sales Success

Timothy Polk, M.A.

Most employees and organizations share a common misconception that no actual "selling" happens during a tradeshow. The exhibit is, they believe, simply a marketing tool designed to distribute brochures or catalogs and "show the flag" to current customers and potential prospects.

But savvy organizations discount this "marketing only" thinking altogether. Instead, they focus on an overlooked but potentially powerful aspect of successful exhibiting at tradeshows: selling while on the show floor.

There are three main aspects to a successful tradeshow selling approach:

1. Knowing and communicating the organization's goals

2. Interacting with customers and prospects

3. Creating specific next steps

Each of these will be covered throughout this chapter.

What You Want to Accomplish

No real "selling" happens during a tradeshow, right? Wrong!

Your organization, its employees, and the products and services you have are constantly "on sale" during a tradeshow. Visitors to your booth are always viewing what they see—consciously and unconsciously—with a view to possibly purchasing the products or services at some point in the future.

There are two connected concepts important to tradeshow selling:

1. While different products and services have different lead times for a sale to occur, in general the sales process is a long one. What's more, it begins when the customer first enters the booth (or even sees it from the aisle!).

2. An actual sale in the form of a customer writing a check or providing a purchase order number doesn't have to happen at the show, but all of the activities at the show should be directed at making a sale happen as soon as possible/feasible after the show.

The following are ways to create, before the show begins, an atmosphere and an attitude among employees that selling does happen, and is important, at a show:

- **Management should agree on sales goals for the show well in advance of the exhibit**. The organization's products and services will determine the amount and type of sales possible. A company which sells $10 employee training manuals, for example, will have many more sales during the show in terms of numbers (but not necessarily dollars) than an organization selling system-wide computer networking services. But the company selling system-wide networking services may connect with one large buyer who, within, three months, places a million dollar order.

- **Each aspect of the organization's exhibit program should be linked, with a common goal of facilitating the sales process.** The booth, hand-out materials, products displayed, excitement-generators used, etc. all should be integrated so that booth visitors and customers are not confused about what it is the organization does, and the products and services it provides.

- **Management should present sales goal information and sales training to booth personnel during pre-show meetings or training sessions.** These training and information exchange sessions will reinforce to employees that they should always be conscious of the sales process and what they can do to promote sales.

The following are important ideas and concepts that will promote the sales process during the show:

- **Don't have employees try to do too much.** The average length of time a customer will spend in any one booth is approximately three to five minutes. Thus, attempting to sell every visitor a complex or expensive—or even simple—product or service is difficult, if not impossible. Instead, the goals of everyone in the organization should be to (1) gather as much information as possible about the customer and his or her needs, and (2) establish a specific follow-up in the future. (Each of these topics is discussed later in this chapter.)

- **Different employees will have different roles.** Entry level or less experienced employees should either focus on distributing marketing materials to unqualified or "browser" visitors, or assist with sales of basic, easy-to-understand products. Account representatives and more experienced employees should speak with, and attempt to sell, higher end customers.

KEY POINT   At key trade shows, an organization may want to leave inexperienced employees at the home office because the potential damage that they may create in terms of confusing or alienating a prospect or client usually far outweighs the advantages of having them in attendance. In addition, show "rookies" usually concentrate far too much on handing out material in an effort to look busy and productive. This discourages meaningful conversations with customers, and the rookie may literally give away important company information to competitors.

- **Different customers will have different needs.** Some customers are not prospects for a variety of reasons: their organization may be too small or they are simply browsing the floor in search of general information. Little time should be spent with these visitors. People from large organizations or current customers, on the other hand, should be given special attention. Those unfamiliar with the organization should be given a brief "tour" of the company's philosophies and key products. Existing customers can be told about new products, exhibit specials, or coming attractions.

- **Use the time crunch to your advantage.** I have seen organizations experience tremendous success with scheduling meetings during shows with key clients or prospects. Clients usually feel much less pressured and the conversation can be more in-depth. Please note, however, that this only works if there is a convenient, quiet spot to meet, such as a designated quiet section of the booth or at a nearby coffee stand.

Interacting with Customers

Once the show doors open, three general things *ideally* should happen with every visitor who enters the booth:

1. The visitor is greeted professionally and courteously.

2. Booth staff should ask questions to learn about the customer and their needs.

3. If the visitor is a legitimate qualified prospect and has a definite need, booth staff should suggest a "solution" in the form of a specific next step.

The Greeting

Greeting a visitor correctly is important for several reasons. Not only do you want the customer to feel welcome, you want her to have a positive first impression of the organization. Employees should do the following to create a positive first impression:

- Look visitors in the eye, smile, and shake hands if appropriate.

- Use the person's name if possible (most name badges have the first name prominently displayed).

- Offer a simple welcoming phrase, such as, "Thank you for visiting our booth," or, "Thanks for stopping by today."

Learning Who, What, and Why

Because time is so short at a show, it is imperative that booth representatives learn as much as possible, in a discreet way, about the visitor. Key answers to learn include:

- The person's name (who)

- The organization they work for (what)

- Their job or role (why)

It is this final element, the 'why,' that is usually the most important piece of information. Learning about the person's job function or role within their organization and a little about why they are at the booth will help you uncover their *need*, a problem or challenge at work that they need help resolving. Only after a prospect's need (problem) has been uncovered can a solution be offered in the form of a product or service.

KEY POINT   Tradeshow selling is no different than everyday selling: the focus of every sale must be matching a solution your organization has to a customer's need or problem.

As you have probably noticed, *questions* are the primary way to learn information about customers and their needs. Questions are critical to successful sales: not only do they get people talking about themselves, they send a subtle message to the customer that you care about them and their needs.

There are two main types of questions: *open-ended questions* and *closed-ended questions*. Both are important to understand and use.

Closed-ended questions can be answered with a "yes" or "no," or by a simple statement of fact. They provide a minimum of feedback. Use closed-ended questions early in a conversation with a customer to narrow down quickly who they are, what organization they work for, and their work role. Examples:

> *"I don't think we've met. My name is Tim Polk. And your name is?"*
>
> *"What organization do you work for?"*
>
> *"What is your title?"*
>
> *"What is your role within the organization?"*
>
> *"Are you familiar with our organization and products?"*

These must be asked, of course, in a natural way—a visitor should never feel that they are being interviewed or "grilled."

Open-ended questions can't be answered with a "yes" or "no"—they require the customer to describe, explain, or otherwise provide more information. Open-ended questions are extremely useful for learning about a customer's needs. Examples:

> *"What are some of the challenges you are facing at the moment?"*
>
> *"Can you tell me a little about how you've used our products before..."*
>
> *"What needs around (the organization's products) do you and your organization have at the moment?"*

"Why are you attending this show?"

"Why are you visiting our booth?"

To get the most benefit from asking questions, booth staffers must be excellent listeners. Only by careful listening can one learn the client's exact needs. Follow these suggestions to become a better listener:

- **Pay attention!** Focus on what the customer is saying, not on what has been said or what you plan to say.

- **Make regular eye contact.** This shows the speaker that you are paying attention and are interested in what they are saying.

- **Don't interrupt.** Let people open up, continue, and finish. Often a listener receives the best information after a person has been speaking for several minutes.

- **Take notes if necessary.** Again, this demonstrates your interest in what the speaker is saying. These notes will help you later during the solution phase.

- **Don't act impatient.** This is difficult, especially if the customer begins to ramble or the booth is swarming with other visitors. But savvy booth personnel act relaxed and comfortable even during the busiest times. Avoid things such as looking at your watch or crossing your arms against your chest.

- **Ask questions if you don't understand what has been said.** Keep asking until you are completely clear what the customer needs, and why.

Once you have learned a little about the customer and their need or needs, two things will be apparent:

- Your organization does NOT have a solution to the customer's need.

- Your organization CAN help the customer.

For the visitor who isn't a good "fit" with your organization's products and services, simply thank the customer for their time and invite them to continue to browse.

For the visitor who does have a legitimate need or problem that your organization can help solve, the booth representative should attempt to move the sales process forward by attempting to solve their problem.

Solving Problems

Up to now the customer has probably been doing most of the talking. But now it's the booth rep's turn to lead the conversation toward a product or service your organization has that will meet the customer's need. Offer a solution this way:

- **State what you feel will help the customer**. Explain as briefly as possible the product and why it will help solve the customer's problem. Use *features* (facts about the product) as little as possible; instead, stress *benefits* (how the customer will benefit from owning the product).

- **Offer support information.** Provide visual aides such as brochures, flyers, catalogs, or videos *that are appropriate*. Give a (brief) product demonstration. Use testimonials from customers with similar or related needs.

- **Keep the customer involved.** Ask them questions such as, "Do you see the benefits of this product?" or "Have you seen this or something similar before?" Whenever possible, have the customer actually test the product. Remember, TRY usually means BUY.

- **Ask for the sale.** The word "sale" in this instance means the customer's belief that the product will more than likely solve their problem or meet their need and that they are interested in continuing (even at a later date) the sales process. The best way to ask for the sale is to simply ask. Examples:

  "Can you see your organization using this product?"

  "Is this something you'd like to utilize (within your department) (at your organization) at some point in the future?"

Listening to the customer's response at this stage of the sales process is critical: some people will be ready, even excited, to move forward, while others will need additional information or resources. Booth representatives should gauge their responses to each individual customer and circumstance.

Specific Next Steps

I have seen countless organizations spend thousands of dollars on booths and travel expenses, and watched employees greet customers, build rapport, and learn all about the customer's needs…and then hand out a business card and catalog and watch the customer walk away from the booth with the customer calling back over his shoulder, "I'll call you later." That's not enough. Why? The customer probably won't call; they'll have visited scores of booths at the show and will soon be (if they already aren't) overwhelmed with information, and after returning to their office they will be inundated with a backlog of work, mail, phone messages and such—in short, they'll be too busy.

In almost every instance, the employee should take the lead in establishing what I call a *quality follow-up*, which is something specific that one or the other (or sometimes both) people will do on or by a specific date. This follow-up is absolutely critical to sales success; without it, much of what has taken place during the booth rep-customer interaction will be wasted.

Examples of a quality follow-up include the following:

- A phone call by one party to the other on a specific day.

- A booth representative faxing or e-mailing pricing information or quote.

- A booth representative mailing additional, more specific information.

- A booth representative making arrangements for the prospect to receive a product preview, sample, or an actual product on a trial basis.

It is imperative that both parties agree what will happen, by whom, and by when *before the customer leaves the booth*. Booth representatives should avoid at all costs the customer who "promises to come back later." Why? The customer might forget, or if they do return it usually is when that particular booth rep is on break or otherwise unavailable.

Once the tradeshow is over, it is equally imperative that the employee follow-up and do exactly what has been promised on or by the designated date. This continues to build trust in the customer's mind and keeps the sales process moving forward.

Summary

Most organizations can reap far greater returns from their tradeshow dollars by emphasizing two important points:

1. Everything related to the booth and staff should be focused on the idea that selling does take place all the time during a show.

2. The sales process is a long one; it does *not* begin and end with the customer entering and then leaving the exhibit.

When employees are trained and coached on the material presented in this chapter, they will have the ability to build sales both at the booth and far after the show.

Timothy Polk, M.A.

Tim Polk is a former million-dollar-a-year Account Manager at Crisp Publications, a northern California publishing company specializing in employee training and development materials. While at Crisp, Tim attended scores of tradeshows and exhibits across the United States, and for two years was the tradeshow manager for Crisp's attendance at the Frankfurt (Germany) Book Fair.

Tim currently has his own writing, editing, and consulting business. Examples of projects he has assisted clients with successfully completing include the following:

- Wrote an employee learning program on the topic of "time management" for a Fortune 1000 organization.

- Edited a book proposal for a Columbus, Ohio, professional speaker that led to multi-agent interest.

- Served as ghostwriter for a book on leadership competencies for a New Jersey entrepreneur.

- Wrote a series of magazine articles for a New Orleans, Louisiana, professional speaker.

- Developed and wrote an employee learning program on the topic of "solution selling" for an organization with more than 400 distributors nationwide.

The author of the books *How to Outlive Your Lifetime!* and *Retail Sales Success,* Tim's essays and articles have appeared in, among others, the San Jose *Mercury News, Washington Living* magazine, *Bay Area Parent,* and the California Bay Area chapter newsletter of The American Society for Training & Development.

Tim frequently travels across the United States and is readily accessible by phone and e-mail. Please contact Tim today to discuss your needs.

Contact information:
Tim Polk
Tel: 707-568-7322
E-mail: POLKpar72@aol.com

SUCCESS

Secret #11

The ABCs of CMI

by
Anne Barron, CME

The ABCs of CMI

Anne Barron, CME

One more secret for successful exhibit marketing is to ensure your program includes Competitive Market Intelligence (CMI).

Trade shows are ideal for:

a) finding new customers,

b) shortening the sales cycle, and

c) introducing new products and services.

Trade shows are a unique marketing medium because they:

a) are three dimensional,

b) allow for two-way exchange of information, and

c) are both marketing and sales.

As a result, trade shows are also ideal for gathering CMI. Some of the best primary-source data you'll ever find is at trade shows and conferences, yet almost all of it goes uncollected.

The North American trade show industry is growing at 10% a year (50% in the computer and electronics industries) according to recent figures from *Tradeshow Week*. If you're not using trade shows to collect data and observe industry trends, you should. A carefully organized data collection plan is needed to gather primary information at shows and conferences, to provide insights that give your firm a competitive edge, and insight into your competitors marketing activities at shows.

Many marketing departments have difficulty justifying exhibit marketing budgets to senior management. The Center for Exhibition Industry Research (CEIR) noted the following in its *An Analysis of the Attitudes and Perceptions of Senior Level Executives Currently Not Utilizing Exhibitions*:

Senior level executives' main objections to trade shows are:

a) **Cost.** Executives are concerned about perceived high costs of trade shows and the inability to demonstrate a reasonable or fair return on investment (ROI).

b) **Difficulty reaching the target market.** Executives are questioning whether the target market actually visits the booth.

c) **Limited contacts due to insufficient processing of leads.** Where are our leads and what is happening to them?

d) **Poor attendance or a crowded, hectic atmosphere.**

e) **The show being unsuitable for the product or services displayed.** Many executives question the show selection and choice process within their organizations.

Executives without strong negative or positive feelings about exhibiting in trade shows cited the unsuitability of exhibitions for their specific business or a difficulty in measuring the impact as reasons for their neutrality.

Include CMI in your exhibit marketing program to further justify your exhibit marketing activities and budget and to measurably show senior level executives the true value and ROI of including trade shows in your strategic marketing program.

Recent research conducted by ABComm Ltd. indicated that most firms interviewed use trade shows to gather some form of CMI, but do little with this information. They do not analyze or share it with others within their organizations. Is your organization guilty of this? If so, you are missing a primary opportunity to gather current information from customers and competitors to enable your firm to identify industry trends and opportunities, i.e., Strengths, Weaknesses, Opportunities and Threats (SWOTs). Information by itself is of no real value. The value of information is what you do with it.

Trade shows provide an ideal forum to gather real time CMI from competitors and customers alike because:

a) you can personally meet and interview new customers, industry leaders, competitors *and their customers,*

b) most exhibitors are introducing new products and services, and

c) most exhibitor staff have not been trained to protect corporate intelligence.

To develop and implement a successful CMI program at trade shows, you'll need to:

a) plan for your success,

b) train your staff to gather and protect CMI, and

c) gather, share and analyze all information.

A) Plan for Your Success

You'll need to coordinate the collection effort on site at the show. To use trade shows successfully in your competitive market intelligence gathering, you must have a plan to gather the information, and more importantly, processes in place to analyze and share the information with key groups in your organization.

Before you get to the show, identify both your key competitors and the information you want to gather. Select no more than five competitors. While you may have a long list of information that you want to gather, prioritize the information and focus in on five key pieces of information you want to gather or verify. Why five? There is only so much time you have to visit your competitors and you can't possibly stay all day asking questions and gathering information. As well, most shows are small and you might be easily detected if you stay too long or ask too many questions at the booth.

Information can be gathered by attending and observing conference sessions, media rooms, booths, networking events, industry publications, show guides, and conference programs, etc. In addition to primary information, you can pick up "intuitive" information to further support your observations. For example, what was the body language or reaction when you asked the question? Did the speaker speak with confidence or seem hesitant?

Meet at least once a day to review information gathered, identify what still needs to be done, and identify any new trends. Summarize this information for sharing in daily show team meetings.

Patience and Observation

Since most individuals with exhibit marketing responsibilities are attending to show logistics, it's important to make time to observe and monitor your activities in comparison to those of your key competitors.

Relatively simple monitoring and observation can reveal valuable information to help your team formulate strategies for upcoming shows and events. Traffic analysis, contact and exposure studies can reveal startling information. Here is a brief list of things you and your staff can gather discreetly at shows:

1. Record competitors booth size, height, etc.

2. Check the show guide for competitors' booth descriptions to see how they are positioning themselves.

3. Take pictures of the booth (always ask for permission).

4. Pick up their literature and gifts or note it.

5. Note their key messages.

6. Interview staff.

7. Gather all show magazines to look for ads and articles. Check local papers for ads and media coverage.

8. Monitor their activities with regard to show sponsorships, e.g., coffee breaks, meals, tote bags, banners, on-site advertising, banners, etc.

9. Review the conference program and plan to attend all sessions presented by your competitors. Observe and record the number of attendees and monitor the interest and questions. Pick up a copy of the handouts. What was the mood of the audience? How did the speakers handle difficult questions? Here you can gather really interesting information, particularly if the speakers are noted for their "off-the-cuff" remarks.

10. Attend networking/social events to monitor what people are saying.

11. Use conference shuttle buses to "mingle" with the crowds and pick up information.

12. Stay at the conference hotels where you are most likely to meet delegates and visitors.

13. Gather press releases. Note that some shows only allow certified press to access the media room.

Visiting the Competition

When visiting the competition, there are some rules of etiquette and professionalism to consider when gathering CMI. The Society of Competitive Intelligence Professionals (SCIP) has a code of ethics, which stresses that **you should never misrepresent your organization or yourself.** Also, don't spend too much time at their booth monopolizing their staff, particularly during busy times.

Since most exhibitors do not approach exhibit marketing from a CMI viewpoint, their booth design and lack of staff training make it fairly easy to gather key information, such as brochures, at their booths. *In most cases*, if you approach and ask questions first, you will be in control to gather information before they qualify you.

Protecting Corporate Intelligence

While information at a trade show is in the "public domain," take a few minutes to review your current program. Is your exhibit marketing program designed to protect your corporate intelligence? Too often the booth design allows your competitors easy access to information. Monitor your activities and security programs during set up and tear down and after show hours. Do not simply walk away from your booth in the evening. Ensure everything is secure. Exhibitors use the quiet times just before and after show hours to gather CMI.

Third Party Analysis

If you already have a CMI team that monitors your performance and that of your competitors at shows, consider hiring an outside agency to gather information for you. This technique is frequently used to verify your information. For example, what happens if you ask a question when you clearly identify yourself as a key competitor compared to the same question being asked by a potential customer or anonymous visitor? Are visitors treated differently and given different information depending on who they are? Bring in a third party agency to get an unbiased, objective view as well as much needed expertise and resources for your program.

B) Train your Staff to Gather and Protect CMI

Train your staff to identify your key competitors, gather appropriate information, *and protect Corporate Intelligence at shows*. **Why make it easy for competitors to gather CMI on your organization?**

There are two groups that need to be trained, your booth staff and the CMI staff who will visit competitor booths. Both groups can gather pertinent information from visitors and competitors in your booth and from staff *and customers* in competitor booths. Employees should also gather and share information collected at shows they attend, but which you are not currently exhibiting.

Gathering CMI at trade shows is relatively easy. Most visitors at a show are in an open and receptive mode. They are attending in order to network and learn. In most cases, they are willing to answer questions or participate in brief surveys, if they feel their participation will lead to a potential new solution to their challenges and concerns. They are very willing to exchange ideas. Train your staff to qualify visitors to the booth and other people they meet at the show. Train them to control the conversation by asking key questions and monitoring their responses to visitor's questions. Who says you have to answer all questions asked?

CEIR studies indicate that 85% of exhibitors do not train their staff. Most booth staff are not aware of either the corporate objectives for the event or their roles in the booth. Consequently, many of these staff are in a "party" mood or upset with their employers for putting them in an unfamiliar and uncomfortable environment. When you toss in alcohol at social events, you've got an opportunity to have casual conversations peppered with probing questions. Often, attendees and exhibitors alike will gratefully answer any and all questions asked. Some employees will innocently or spitefully share corporate intelligence with competitors. Can your organization afford this?

As previously discussed, most exhibitors and executives underestimate the tremendous business and sales opportunities at stake at industry shows and events. They do not train their staff to protect corporate intelligence or anticipate competitors. Train your staff to protect corporate intelligence, recognize competitors, and gather valuable, real-time CMI that will help your organization stay competitive and anticipate all strengths, weaknesses, opportunities and threats (SWOTs).

C) Gather, Analyze and Share Information

The major challenge for most exhibitors is not gathering CMI, but analyzing and sharing it. Before you arrive at the show, have the processes in place to ensure that all information gathered is forwarded to one centralized location for evaluation. Condense all information into an "executive" summary format for distribution to the team. Include your observations of your booth and of your competitors, major recommendations, and the potential benefits.

You will be amazed at the information and trends you can identify when you develop and implement a strategy to gather and monitor CMI. Here are a few examples:

a) **Situation:** An exhibitor was able to determine that their primary competitor got more exposure from a lesser sponsorship category. **Result:** the exhibit manager recommended that show management be contacted for explanation and to receive guarantee that this would not happen again. **Benefit:** exhibitor got premium exposure and show management prevented this problem at future events.

b) **Situation:** An exhibitor identified their primary competitor was not exhibiting, but had a high profile at the event. **Result:** the exhibit manager was able to anticipate their presence at the show the following year and recommended a stronger presence in order to maintain market position. **Benefit:** Exhibitor was able to maintain leadership role at industry event.

c) **Situation:** An exhibitor identified that their primary key competitor had a very aggressive media strategy and that they had been preparing for the show at least three months in advance with great success. **Result:** the exhibit manager recommended that a strong media campaign needed to be implemented early in order to ensure their story got covered. **Benefit:** Exhibitor was better prepared and budgeted for media coverage.

d) **Situation:** An exhibitor analyzed their return on investment (ROI) and compared it to that of key competitors. **Result:** exhibitor was able to show senior management that budgets were well in line with key competitors and that they had a stronger presence and better ROI than competitors. **Benefit:** senior management were impressed with the information and more money was allocated to the trade show program.

e) **Situation:** An exhibitor was able to identify that a key competitor was getting ready to enter a new market and could be a potential threat to future market share. **Result:** exhibitor was prepared to counter the move and had a year to plan. **Benefit:** it prevented a "surprise" to senior management.

The report should allow for comparison of information from show to show and year to year so that trends can be identified and recommendations made to senior management. Just giving them information is not good enough. Information in and of itself has no value. It's what you do with the information that brings value to your organization. Depending on the information you gather, your report can be a useful tool for show selection, booth staffing, products/services to display, etc.

The benefits to you and your organization for including a CMI program as part of your exhibit marketing program are countless. Including a CMI program will help "take the guesswork out of exhibit marketing'" for your organization and senior level executives. They will become believers in the true value of trade shows in the marketing mix.

Anne Barron, CME

Anne Barron, CME is President of ABComm™ Ltd. This Certified Manager of Exhibits (CME) has more than a decade of experience in the field. Anne has developed, implemented and managed award winning corporate exhibit and marketing programs for some of Canada's leading telecommunications and high technology companies. She has served as President of the Association of Professional Exhibitors of Canada (APEC). She is a member of and has served on Board committees of the Trade Show Exhibitors Association (TSEA) and Center for Exhibition Industry Research. She also served on the TSEA Board of Directors for three years.

Anne has published numerous articles and is frequently quoted in trade show industry publications. She also presents an annual series of exhibit marketing seminars to corporate executives across North America.

Over the years, Anne has been recognized internationally by her peers with an number of awards for her outstanding performance. These include a Grand Award from the Trade Show Exhibitors Association, a first place award from AFCEA (Armed Forces Communications and Electronics Association), an advertising award for IABC (International Association of Business Communicators) and an individual award from the Partners in Education program of the Ottawa-

Carleton Learning Foundation. She is frequently invited to judge booth design and exhibits at TSEA, EDAC, etc.

Anne has also been recognized as an outstanding entrepreneur by being nominated for Canada's Entrepreneur of the Year by Nesbitt Burns. She was a finalist in Trimark's 1998 Canadian Women's Mentor of the Year program and has been featured in *Chatelaine Magazine,* the *Ottawa Citizen* and the *Ottawa Sun.*

ABComm™ Ltd.

ABComm™ Ltd., "takes the guesswork out of exhibit marketing" with complete and strategic exhibit planning, management and consultation services. It has over 15 years experience in developing and implementing strategic exhibit marketing programs that can be measured. A key component of these programs is gathering, analyzing, and sharing competitive market intelligence through show research and on-site analysis at shows. ABComm provides an objective, third party perspective.

Other services include:

- In-depth show research and evaluation
- Developing RFPs for the purchase of new booths, including needs analysis
- Developing and implementing strategic exhibit marketing programs that get measurable results
- On-site booth and staff management
- On-site performance and competitive analysis
- Developing and implementing CMI programs
- Booth staff training in English, French and Spanish
- Providing booth staff
- Managing show logistics
- Developing and implementing simple, effective lead management programs
- Special events

- Developing private label awards, recognition, and incentive programs for corporate gift giving to customers and employees.

Our training programs include full day basic workshops in strategic exhibit marketing for those individuals responsible for the day to day management of exhibit marketing programs and advanced programs for senior managers, directors, Vice-Presidents, etc., wishing to implement programs that get measurable results.

For more information on ABComm Ltd. and our services visit our web site

www.AB-Comm.com

or contact us at:

1069 Arnot Road
Ottawa, Ontario
K2C 0H5
Tel. (613) 224-0447
FAX (613) 224-3826
Anne can be reached at abarron@ab-comm.com.

Exhibit Management and Education
Gestion de stands d'exposition et formation

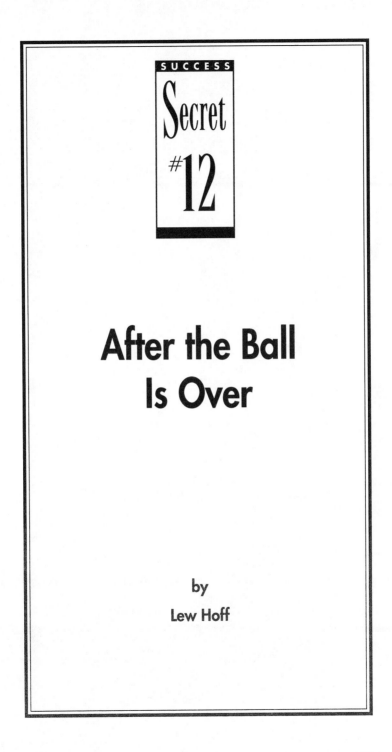

SUCCESS

Secret #12

After the Ball Is Over

by
Lew Hoff

After the Ball Is Over

Lew Hoff

If your first thoughts about tradeshow sales lead follow-up occur only as work crews start furiously rolling up the carpets and tearing down exhibits around you, you are, in the words of my nine-year-old, "dead meat." If you haven't given serious thought as to how you will successfully follow-up the tradeshow leads that you've just collected, your company has just invested a lot of money for which its return, if any, will be based purely on luck.

Prepare

Effective tradeshow follow-up begins long before the last business card is exchanged, long before the last farewell to your fellow exhibitors. Follow-up preparation begins *before* the tradeshow and continues as the show progresses. To a great extent, by the time you depart the show, the die has been cast. If you have prepared well in advance and executed your plan during the show, then many of your sales leads will result in sales, or better yet, in decade-plus customers.

Set goals

Going into a show you must have written goals. Showing the flag is *not* a goal. ("We've got to be there: all our competitors will be attending, and people will think something is wrong if we don't show up.") Acquiring new customers is. Regaining lost customers is a good goal. Retaining current customers is as well. We can apply quantifiable measures to each of these goals, such as sales revenues from new sources over "x" number of months after the show. Simply showing up is not going to assure that you will meet your goals. Yes, you have to do a good job at the show. But few tradeshow attendees place orders on the spot. Most make their buying decisions in the days, weeks and months following a tradeshow. Do you want to leave your prospects buying decisions to chance? Effective follow-up is required if you are going to meet ambitious goals.

Your system

The ability to follow-up on tradeshow leads is dictated by the manner in which the leads are collected. If your "system" is to ask for a business card on the back of which you make a few notations, you will have a lot of key entry to do and you will have to work on assumptions for which there may be no foundation. What assumptions? You will not have the demographic information that is typically encoded on a tradeshow attendee's badge. You will have to ask for or do without key qualifiers, such as:

1. Type of business

2. Number of locations

3. Annual sales

4. Number of employees

5. Level of decision-making authority of the badge holder

6. Purpose for attending the show

Electronic lead management

If you will employ an electronic lead management system at your tradeshow, acquaint yourself with its features prior to the show. Some of these features could prove very helpful to you in your follow-up phase. For example, if your organization is promoting multiple products or services at a tradeshow, wouldn't it be useful if you could break down your leads by product or service? Perhaps you would like to pass on leads to sales representatives based on assigned geographical territories; in that case, an automated breakdown by postal ZIP code would expedite matters. The ability to download your leads to your contact management or customer relationship management database is particularly useful.

Qualifiers

One important benefit of electronic lead management is its ability to attach qualifiers to each of your leads. Some systems contain a limited number of fixed qualifiers, such as "hot lead," "send salesman," "send literature" etc. Other systems have a series of buttons, usually between four and ten. You, the user, define the qualifier for each. Then there are systems that provide generic qualifiers, along with the ability to write a large number of user defined qualifiers. Whatever system you use, the inclusion of qualifiers will enhance your ability to follow-up effectively on leads.

Qualifying your prospects is a key element in your tradeshow follow-up process. Here are the five "W's" on which to focus:

1. **Who** are they?

2. **What** caused them to attend the show? What caused them to visit your exhibit?

3. **Why** will your product address their need?

4. **Where** do they stand in the decision making process?

5. **When** does their need require fulfillment?

Your goal is, or should be, to turn prospects into decade-plus customers. To do that you have to be able to differentiate your product/service and to add value to your customer's product/service.

Who? For each lead you need to know:

1. Name

2. Title

3. Organization

4. Type of business

5. Address

6. Telephone

7. Fax and e-mail number

You may have had a dozen visitors to your exhibit or thousands. Determining just who your visitors are is the first step in qualifying them. The name of the company with which they are affiliated may offer an indication of their interest. Your visitor could be a competitor. (Before you simply discard this type of "lead," you might want to consider a few points raised under "why?" He or she could be with a company with whom you might want to form a strategic alliance.)

Who does your visitor represent? A Fortune 500 firm? An Internet hotshot? A multi-national? A firm on the rise or on the decline? A company that you can grow with, or a Goliath to your David?

Why? Why did your lead attend this event? If she was looking for products/services like those that you offer, you clearly have a prime prospect. If she was there to gain competitive intelligence, that puts her at the other end of the spectrum. In between there are people who attended the event for any number of reasons. Perhaps related seminars were of the greatest interest. Or related products. Or networking. Knowing the reason is important to you in qualifying your leads.

Why did the lead visit your exhibit? Perhaps a current customer referred her. That makes her a particularly well-qualified prospect. Your visitor might not have a need for your product, but she might know someone who does. Even a visitor from a competitor does not have to be unwelcome. He may be an excellent source of information on mutual competitors. Or he might be someone with an ego, the type that gives you inside dope on his company in order to burnish his image as an insider. There could be any one of a number of reasons why someone visits you. Find the one.

If she came specifically because of an interest in using your product or service, why? Business people do not buy products or services, they buy solutions to problems.

What? What is the problem that your visitor hopes to solve? What can you offer as a solution?

Defining the problem that your prospect hopes to solve is not always straightforward. For example, he might say, "My problem is that our air compressor is only 15 horsepower. Our usage has grown. I need something bigger." Maybe he does. Or maybe he simply has the wrong type of compressor. A newer, more efficient model of the same capacity might serve him quite well, while reducing his energy consumption. His problem could be that he does not have a drier to dry the air that the compressor is using, resulting in excessive moisture that is causing mechanical damage. If your response is to simply send him a quote on a 25 horsepower compressor to replace his "inadequate" 15 horsepower unit, you may lose the sale to a more inquisitive salesperson.

Before you can offer a solution, you have to thoroughly understand the problem. If you want a long-term customer, one that I call a "decade-plus customer," your goal has to be one of mutual satisfaction, not simply a sale. You must give the customer a real solution, one that will look as good, or even better, a year down the road.

Add value. When following up on a lead, focus on this question: What can I offer this prospect that will add value to his product or service and help differentiate it from those of his competitors? You may not have been able to sufficiently analyze his problem on the spot on the tradeshow floor. In the follow-up phase you have the opportunity to do this and to offer the value add that will begin a "decade-plus customer" relationship.

Where? Where does your exhibit visitor stand in the decision making process within his or her organization? We all want to deal with decision makers, but not everyone in an organization is a decision maker. Those who are not can fall into one of a number of categories:

1. The **advocate** is a person who has the both the standing within his organization and the passion to influence those who do make the decisions.

2. The **wise old man** is a fixture at the organization. He is part historian, part muse, someone who may have survived by going along but knows the business. He word usually carriers weight.

3. The **gadfly** flutters around at each tradeshow finding things of interest, none of which he will care about once the show is over and he

is back at his office. He has little standing within his organization.

When? When will a decision be made on the product/service that you are offering? The answer plays a large part in how you prioritize your leads. To whom do you devote your energies right now, the Fortune 500 lead who plans to purchase in 18 months, or the three-year-old outfit with $2 million in sales with an immediate need?

If your company is firmly established and a leader in its field, your outlook is quite different than that of an entrepreneur in the early stages of growth. Sure, the entrepreneur would like to grab some of Mr. Fortune 500's business, but, hey, 18 months out? For a start-up, that is an eternity. The lifeblood of a start-up is cash, and cash comes from sales.

Garbage in, garbage out

Many of these questions will be answered as you capture and qualify leads during the course of your tradeshow. Whether you use a paper-based lead qualification system or an electronic lead management system, the old computer dictum applies: Garbage in, garbage out. If you do not employ the right lead qualifiers, you will not get the right information. Sure, the demographic information that you can capture from an encoded visitor badge will help immensely by forming the foundation of the demographic data. But you have the opportunity to get answers to questions that are not included in the registration. Seize that opportunity.

Use the Web

After the show, you have to fill in the blanks. Get answers to questions that could not be covered under demographics or the lead qualifiers. The most obvious place to begin to fill in the blanks is the prospect's Web site. Depending on the content on the prospect's Web site, you might not have to go any further for prospect intelligence.

If your lead has no Web site or one with very little information, you can turn to other resources on the Web. If your prospect is a public company, the Security and Exchange Commission offers a great deal of on-line information. For privately held companies you will have to dig harder, but with the Web, it is unlikely that you will come up empty handed.

Leads are highly perishable

Do not let the qualified leads you have assembled languish. They are gold—but perishable gold. Leads grow old quickly. Stephen Covey, author of *The 7 Habits of Highly Effective People,* divides tasks into four categories: Urgent and important; important and not urgent; urgent and not important; not urgent and not important. Done properly, tradeshow preparation should be "important and not urgent"—it should be done well in advance of the show. Lead follow-up is both important and urgent.

Three-phase follow-up

In your follow-up, as in a speech, tell them what you are going to tell them, tell them, then tell them what you told them. Don't expect a one shot follow-up to produce results.

Too frequently an exhibitor's follow-up, if you can call it that, consists of nothing more than a single piece of literature with a "personal" cover letter. Don't kid yourself. That isn't follow-up.

Set yourself and your organization apart from the crowd

Start with an e-mail message or brief letter thanking your prospect for having visited your exhibit. Explain to him that more information will follow shortly. Give him a preview of the coming attractions. Tell him what you are going to tell him.

Five to seven days later, send a second e-mail or letter accompanied by an attachment or enclosures. Provide your prospect with a value add, either a solution to his problem or a means of differentiating his product or service. Close with a call for action. Since your initial point of contact was a tradeshow, you might instill a sense of urgency by offering some type of show special, some inducement for him to act now. This is the "tell him" phase.

In another five to seven days, tell him what you've told him. Send an e-mail or letter recapping the benefits your organization is prepared to deliver that will solve problems or differentiate products. Offer a compelling reason to act now. Tell him what you told him.

Get personal

Do not rely strictly on the written word, be it by e-mail, fax or snail mail. If you have a few dozen leads, you should also be able to conduct a telephone campaign. If you have hundreds of leads, you may have enough people on staff to allow for rapid follow-up by telephone. If you have lots of leads but not lots of people, you have decisions to make. Some leads will be more urgent than others. Clearly, a lead bearing the qualifier "immediate need" calls for a quick response, especially so if there is the potential for a large order or for a long-term relationship.

Your ten to twenty day "tell them" written follow-up campaign has to kick-in to a more personal phase within 30 days after the tradeshow concludes. Prime prospects, as you defined them when you planned your tradeshow participation, should be contacted by telephone or in person within that 30-day window.

Keep at it

No athlete, no matter how talented, wins every game, nor does any athletic team win 'em all. But great players and great teams learn from their losses and come back to win another day. So, too, for the successful salesperson. The leads that do not pan out following this year's tradeshow should not be assigned to the scrap heap. Many of the same folks will attend the same show next year and the year after. Some will move up within their company. They will become decision-makers. Others will move on, seeking more fertile pastures. While your product did not go over at their previous organization, it might be just what their new company needs. Continue to work the leads that did not result in a sale. Some (OK—maybe most) will eventually be discarded after a period of years. But others might become decade-plus customers.

Summary

As an exhibitor, you have made a substantial investment. Just add up the cost of salaries, exhibit space, your display, travel, food, lodging and entertainment and I am sure that you will agree. Preparation, execution and above all lead follow-up are the elements that will assure that you will realize a substantial return on investment.

Lew Hoff

Lew Hoff is the president of Bartizan Data Systems, a spin-off of Bartizan Corporation, of which he is also president. Bartizan Corporation has been manufacturing data collection devices for the credit card industry since 1970. Its customers include major financial institutions worldwide. Hoff is a member of the Board of the Hudson Valley Technology Development Center and is president of the Westchester World Trade Council.

Bartizan Data Systems is a developer and manufacturer of tradeshow sales lead management systems. Bartizan lead management systems are available worldwide exclusively through its network of tradeshow registration contractors. These systems can be rented, leased or purchased by registration contractors. The Bartizan Box has been used at tradeshows throughout North America, in Latin America, Australia and in Europe.

Bartizan devotes considerable resources to tradeshow sales lead management. Nearly half of its 39,000 square foot facility located just outside of New York City is devoted to this segment of its business. A product development staff of seven engineers works on refining current products, as well as developing new ones. Bartizan's Board of Directors includes the Dean of Engineering at New York Institute of Technology and former IBM executives.

The Bartizan Box, as Bartizan's lead management system is known, is a desktop telephone size device that incorporates many features, including: a display; floppy drive; magnetic stripe reader; 3 serial ports; PDF barcode reading capability; thermal printer; 18-key keyboard. It can store 3,000 leads in battery-backed memory and another 3,000 on a floppy disk. It can be operated on standard electrical current worldwide and it can operate off of a battery pack.

To contact Lew Hoff or learn more about
Bartizan and its products:
call 1-800-431-2682
or visit the web site at http:/www.bartizan.com